BRIGHTON

Trans*formed

QueenSpark Books

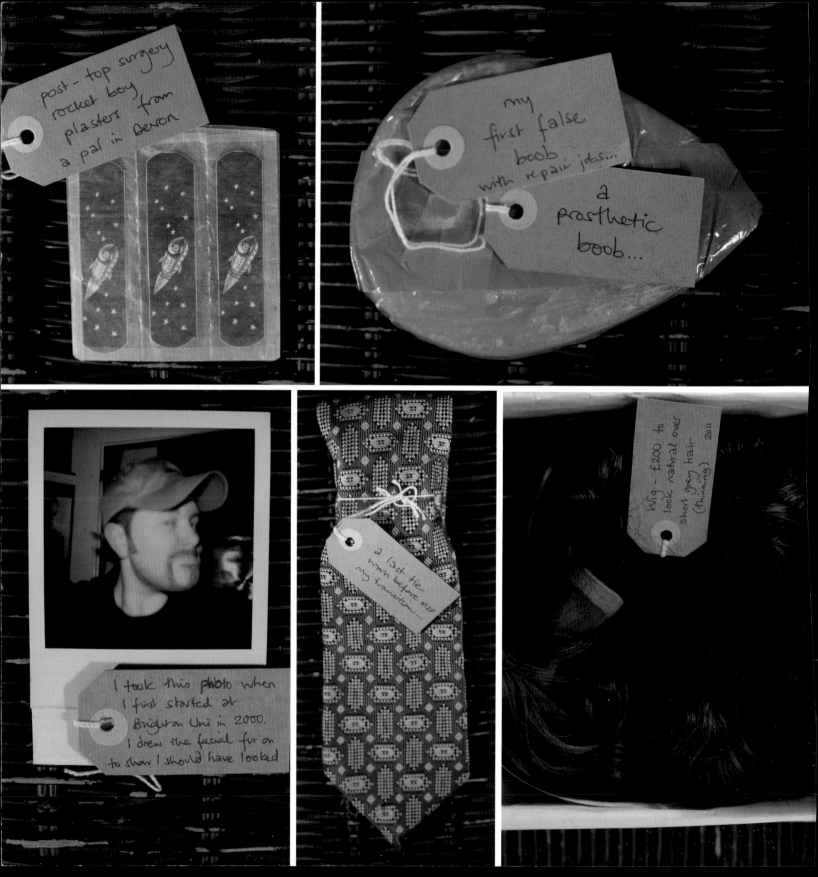

Lindsey, Luke & Michelle "Gender Benders" 80s Brighton

wedding photos

"this reminds my girlfriend of me"

Published by QueenSpark Books, a not for profit community publisher, which, for over 40 years, has helped the people of Brighton & Hove to tell their stories.

QueenSpark Books
Room 207
University of Brighton
10-11 Pavilion Parade
Brighton
BN2 1RA

T: 01273 571710
www.queensparkbooks.org.uk

ISBN 978-0-904733-93-8
A catalogue record of this book is available from the British Library

First published 2014

Printed locally by Gemini Brighton
www.gemini-brighton.co.uk

GEMINI | BRIGHTON

Thanks to the University of Brighton for its support of QueenSpark Books.

heritage lottery fund
LOTTERY FUNDED

Brighton & Hove City Council

The biggest thanks are due to the Brighton Trans*formed interviewees and interviewers who have made this project what it is:
Sabah, Alice Denny, Nick, Ludo Foster, Fox Fisher, Sam Hall, Darcy Heston, Cass Hoskins, Ben, Ruth Rose, Joanna Rowland-Stuart, Sarah Savage, E-J Scott, Stephanie Scott, Rory Finn, Edward, Rebecca Williams, Gloria, Maeve Devine, Luc Raesmith, Reuben, Ezekiel, Eli, Michelle Steele and Kim Curran.

For their work on the Brighton Trans*formed book:
Editor - Dr Sam Carroll
Assistant Editor - Maeve Devine
Book Design - FoxFisher.com
Art Director - Stella Cardus
Design volunteers - Rory Finn, Cass Hoskins, E-J Scott and Luc Raesmith
Juliet Jacques for her introduction
Proof-readers - Helen Walker, John Riches, Catherine Page, Esther Gill, Gerry Holloway, Melita Dennett, Ben Paley, Kathy Caton, Maeve Devine and Sam Carroll.

Photography by Sharon Kilgannon, Alonglines.com, assisted on some shoots by stylist Giulia Carri.

The Brighton Trans*formed Exhibition was curated by:
E-J Scott, working with volunteers Ben, Darcy Heston, Cass Hoskins, Luc Raesmith, and Charly Thieme.

The Exhibition Group would like to thank:
Sharon Kilgannon, Leesifer Frances, Roni Guetta, Kesiena Boom, David, Tarik, Kat, Fynn, and the team at The Marlborough Pub & Theatre, Billie Lewis, Kathy Caton, Brighton Gin and the gin shed, The Wood Store, Judith Galloway, Kirsten Wheatley, Rachael Whitbread and the Jubilee Library, James Robinson and Fifi Pedro Pruen at the Gilded Cage Tattoo Studio, Marion, Rosa Valdez, Leah Organa, the Trans Pride Committee (Sabah, Fox Fisher, Phoenix Thomas, Stephanie Scott, Sarah Savage, Kit Roskelly, Vicki Cook), the Resource Centre, Shabitat, Reprographics, Fitzherberts, The Unitarian Church, and all from The Clare Project and FTM Brighton who contributed to the Cabinet of Memories.

Many thanks to the Brighton Trans*formed Steering Group:
Rory Finn, Dr Sam Hall, Claire Parker, Stephanie Scott, John Riches, Gerry Holloway, Melita Dennett and Kathy Caton.

Project Manager - John Riches
Project Co-ordinator - Kathy Caton
Project Admin - Nicola Benge
Website - Melanie Menard

Special thanks to RadioReverb 97.2fm

Brighton changed so much during my eight years there, and of course it transformed me too.

Foreword: *Juliet Jacques*

I grew up near Brighton & Hove, visiting during my teens in the late 1990s, when the flowering gay and lesbian scene and musical counter-culture helped it move beyond its reputation as another shabby seaside town to become a city for the new millennium.

Both of these attracted me, a twenty-one year old graduate confused about my gender and sexuality, wanting to be back with my old artist and musician friends from Horsham who'd moved to Brighton, rebelling against Home Counties conformism. I came to do my Masters, become a writer and maybe form a band, but my big discovery at the University of Sussex was 'transgender', and then 'trans' - as an identity, as theory and as a community.

I began as 'gay', finding myself as Juliet in the Harlequin nightclub in 2002, with its drag queens and toilets marked 'Women/ TV/TS'. When I moved to Brighton a year later, I began exploring the Kemp Town bars which started calling themselves 'LGBT' rather than 'Gay and Lesbian', and realised that at last, there might be a place for me. Then I was 'transgender' and 'genderqueer' before deciding to transition in 2009 - finding The Clare Project, mentioned many times here, to be an excellent support group.

There, I met some of the people, of various ages, genders, sexualities and races, who feature in Brighton Trans*formed. The 'transition narrative' had become a cliché long before I wrote mine for the Guardian as A Transgender Journey, but life stories are powerful - they help to break down stereotypes and show more ways to lead a gender-variant life, especially when presented as they are in these pages, as a collection of voices which reflect common concerns but also illuminate individual paths. Themes emerge: relationships with the NHS, police, schools and local authorities; how people came to realise their gender identities, and the need for services for them and those around them; how they feel about the LGB community, and how to maintain that alliance, acknowledging that while prejudices against both are interlinked, gender and sexuality are very different things.

Brighton is not here presented as perfect - people discuss issues of race, class and ability in a still very white, middle-class area, transphobia in LGBT spaces and on the streets, and problems with the transitional pathway with services based in London. It is, however, a relatively safe haven for many of us, constantly changing for the better, in some ways quickly, in others slowly. Certainly, it's a place where trans people are increasingly seen and heard, understood and respected - and Brighton Trans*formed shows how far we've come, and how far there is to go.

Contents

Brighton Trans*formed is timely as many believe we are at a 'tipping point' of trans visibility, rights and representation.

Introduction: *Rory Finn & E-J Scott*

Brighton Trans*formed is timely as many believe we are at a "tipping point" of trans visibility, rights and representation.

Trans people in Brighton have a long history, but recently there have been significant developments in how the community connects and organises itself. The last few years have seen it blossom with new groups complementing the stalwart Clare Project. Ranging between peer support (FTM Brighton and Transformers), social (Trans Pride and Trans Swimming Club) and activism (Trans Alliance), these groups have been established and are led by trans-identified people. A perfect time to capture a newly found confidence and preserve the life stories of some of those who make the community what it is.

Our contributors range from 18 to 81 years old and come from varied backgrounds with very different life experiences. All of their testimonies have in common an absolute honesty and openness: contributors let us into some of their most intimate, heart-breaking and heart-warming stories. They shared their joys and tragedies; the adversities they face(d) and all show a discernible strength and resolve to be who we know ourselves to be.

Contributors worked through confidence issues and self-protective boundaries to appear on posters, radio, in public art and this book – all in order to express what being a trans person in Brighton, and arguably universally, is really like. They did this to educate wider society and to support those who are starting their own gender exploration. Many work incredibly hard for the rights of gender variant people and it has been a privilege to preserve all of their stories for future generations and to create role models and prove that we are here!

For over 40 years, QueenSpark Books has been producing books about the people of Brighton & Hove, with a focus on enabling 'lesser-heard' voices to tell their stories. 'Lesser-heard' can sometimes be read as 'ignored', 'shunned', or even 'persecuted', which makes the telling of these stories so important. With Brighton Trans*formed this objective was underlined many times. Even before Heritage Lottery funding was secured, QueenSpark was approached by individuals eager to be involved in a project where editorial and creative control lay firmly with the community it was seeking to represent - a community whose voices have historically been distorted, misrepresented and sensationalised.

A huge number of unpaid and voluntary hours have gone in to delivering this project and the quality of the finished book is an absolute testament to this. The steering committee, our volunteers and staff were made up of local trans folk and allies, ensuring that the project had a golden thread of trans experience and voices throughout. Many of our interviewers were also interviewees, so they understood what a big ask it was to record the testimonies of their peers.

Our narrative is an overriding one of hope not tragedy. We sought to empower and enable the community with opportunities that, by virtue of its trans status and all that this entails, had previously been unforthcoming. We've made friends, raised visibility, shared skills and ultimately, affected significant change. This is what community projects, public art and oral testimony can do. Brighton Trans*formed is the evidence.

Rory Finn grew up in Devon but moved to Brighton at 18 for university. He has lived here ever since. He enjoys making music, playing xbox and drinking tea.

Chapter One: *In Brighton things are shifting.*

Communities, Trans Pride, LGBTQ, differences, support

E-J

I've been a trans man walking the pavements of Brighton – 'promenading' as it was called here back in the early nineteenth century – for over ten years now.

Brighton is a socially aware space. It's a place that has activists, it's got the beach, it's rich in culture and urban landscape. You can walk everywhere and there's a very friendly (albeit small) community here, who I think get along by and large very well because we're all very different people and that fits the feel of the place. I don't find it an angry community, our trans community. I don't find it downtrodden and bitter. I find it quite gay, and I mean gay as in creative and fun, you know, the old fashioned meaning of the word.

The trans community in Brighton is full of hope and there are people standing up who are proud of who they are and where they've come from. And there are people coming out of the woodwork responding to that of all ages, nationalities, shapes and sizes. It's all about where we can go, not so much about how hurt we've been. I think we all take on board that it's going to be up to us to build our community events; to have parties, art exhibitions, meetings; to do theatre, meet and laugh and walk. I walked along the beach the other day, along the cliff faces from Brighton to Rottingdean with a group of friends that I met at The Clare Project. We just had a healthy outdoor time in the sunshine, by the beach in Brighton. We stopped for a cup of tea and a cake. It was just great, we didn't even talk about being trans. Lots of serious advocacy happens in Brighton, but I really do believe it's got that positive energy to it because we've got some great people involved in a community that's set in a very pretty and historically rich place.

I'm not saying that all trans people's experiences here are the same. No way. We're all individuals and we all have different histories and herstories and itstories. But I think that support and talking and friendship and camaraderie is so heart-warming when you're scared and lonely and fearing rejection from everyone around you, especially the people that are closest to you. When you feel like you're going to cause other people to feel shame, or be embarrassed, it's so devastating. Having other trans people around you go, "You don't mean to. That's broader society's problem, not yours. You're not hurting anybody by being transgendered", it's absolutely essential to have partners and friends and support around.

Our trans communities are growing in their profiles, in their reach and in their diversity of messages. It would have made my life a whole lot easier if it had been there when I was transitioning fifteen odd years ago. I was just lucky to have got through, because I really nearly didn't and it still scares me when I think about how far I've come and what it was like back then. It was just horrendous. So we've got to make sure that people network and for those of us who are brave enough to be out, we must speak out, because that's how we're going to break down all the stereotypes and that's how other trans people are going to find themselves.

Alice

I came to Brighton to maintain contact with my friends from The Clare Project and the friends that I had made in Brighton, it was supposed to be a temporary move really, while I got my bearings. Brighton got under my skin, as it does, and it's really only last week that I finally said, I think I've completely committed myself to being in Brighton permanently.

I've still got roots in Hastings, I love Hastings. And although I thought I was trying to find somewhere to live in Brighton, I still held onto that link back there. Then I realised that it wasn't a good idea to try to revisit the past.

Remembering what it was like the last time I had to go back to Hastings for just a few months hiatus, and that was a really desperate time. Almost undid all the good work I'd been doing in Brighton.

I'm not scared of being anywhere else, I just feel really comfortable in Brighton.

I really love my friends in Brighton, they mean more to me than they could imagine. Brighton's encouraged me to perform my poetry rather than just write it and keep it to myself and it gives me avenues for doing the things that I really like doing, spontaneously. Not many places can do that. It's not too big, it's not anonymous. You walk down the street and people know you.

Now I have a lot more men friends, male friends. I say "men friends" it sounds as if I've gone straight or something, but, you know, I've got lots of male friends which I didn't have before. I found it very hard to relate to men in the way that men do. Brighton's just given me this whole new outlook on life and I feel it gives me the chance of expressing the real me.

Ruth

I've been involved with Brighton Council on producing this thing that they developed last year about transgendered people having a positive policy. There were about five or six of us that they consulted at length to get the thing right. They gave us a questionnaire and we had to answer questions and it was just hopeless because it asked questions about "Do we believe that abuse is wrong" and that sort of thing. If you put a wrong answer you were obviously some bad citizen. At the end of it, we sent a message back to the Council. "Next time we'll ask the questions you give us the answer". To their credit the Council woke up. They came back with a positive policy that they had pieced together, they consulted us at length about it. They made a really good job of it.

They're probably the first city to do this sort of thing. To adopt a properly thought out transgender policy which is not just tolerance, but something which is positive. That accepts that this is part of their society and makes provision for it. Also, in Brighton's case, to be quite happy to attract older people who have retired and are transgendered, or going through a transgender process, to come and live in Brighton because it's more tolerant and more positive about these things. That is the sign that they're looking beyond just saying "We've got them here, we've got to look after them", it's saying "Let them come. Let them be here, because we're the place to be". So I'm actually feeling quite buoyant about the community that we have in Brighton.

There's a real split in the community between those who identify as part of the LGBTQI rest of the alphabet community and those who don't who might come from a more straight background. Or may have transitioned and don't feel part of the community anymore because they're identified as straight. Trans T is very much part of the LGBT acronym and I think it's foolish of LGB activists to think that gender doesn't have anything to play in their being trodden on by the rest of the world. So it's all inter-linked and, in my humble opinion, it all comes down to sexism at the end of the day.

I think trans is very much part of the LGBT community, it always has been and it always will be in different ways and in different hues. Queer activism is important for me and quite distinct to gay rights activism in that it's freedom from these labels but it's also very much about the mixing of the sexuality and the gender stuff as well. There is quite a lot of feminism in that too. So it was about doing club nights, educating people at different levels, teaching people top tips about being a trans ally or going into a classroom and training professionals into best practice. A whole range of things.

I ended up doing stuff with the police, talking to them about their stop and search policy, giving them training. I've also ended up kicking Brighton & Hove City Council up the butt and getting them to do something about trans stuff which has led on to this amazing massive bit of work; The Trans Scrutiny Panel. It's not just me doing this on my own, but it's getting involved in little bits and then opportunities come together and you meet people who help and together you get things done.

Every year there's the Trans Day of Remembrance and we do a Sunday service at Dorset Gardens Methodist Church as a community and commemorate the dead. As with most LGBT events in the city it's quite standard to invite politicians to come. Only this year every single politician failed to turn up. This was back in 2011. We quite rightly got a bit upset about that and Nick, Steph and I were sort of meeting on a fairly regular basis to talk about various trans things in the city. At the time I was the chair of FTM Brighton, Steph was chair of The Clare Project and Nick was the co-ordinator of LGBT HIP. We wrote a letter to all the political parties and Phelim Mac Cafferty who is the Green's LGBT rep invited us to a meeting with him and Bill Randall, who at the time was the Leader of the Council.

So we met with Phelim and Bill and had a chat about what the issues were for trans people. They were like, "Well maybe we could do a trans scrutiny" and they explained what it was and a few months later the ball started rolling. Out of it we've had this massive investigation into inequalities faced by trans people in the city. The recommendations got published in January 2013 and there's ongoing work now whereby statutory services, the police, the NHS, the council and others are having to get together and talk about trans people. It's basically completely changed the playing field. Trans people are now being included and mandated. Things are changing for trans people in the city in a really substantial way as a result of that. And that makes me very proud that I was part of the process and that as a community we've been able to effect quite a lot of change.

Rory

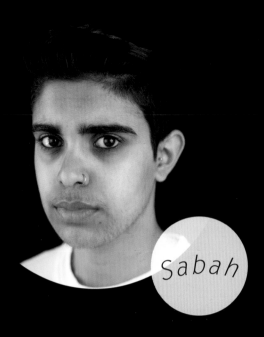

Sabah

It's after seeing what Brighton Pride turned into. A lot of different LGBT people in the city were all a bit displeased and realised that the trans community needs their own thing. A lot has changed in Brighton and Hove, trans people do have a voice. There are things like the Trans Alliance forming and people are changing their policies and implementing things to protect trans people's identities, understanding things. People are calling out transphobia, and it's a really powerful movement that's happening. I think that's emerged with the reclamation of a queer identity, which is really great. But in terms of the gay scene and the trans scene, if there really is one, I think the gay scene is quite dominant, identifying themselves by their sexuality. That's reflective of mainstream society with labelling things, putting things into a box.

Trans itself is an umbrella term for so many different things; it's a gender identity, it's a political identity, it's all sorts of things. I think that's what people find really hard to understand. It's about trying to make people who identify as gay understand and listen and say like "This is your struggle too. We're in this together". Trans Pride can reach out even further than it did last year.

I really want to get the BME communities and more people of colour involved. There's some kind of stereotypes around that need to be broken, even around like the notion that you can't be black and gay. It's really hard to talk about race, especially when you're talking about transphobia and homophobia and biphobia as well. I really want people, when they hear the word 'diversity', to understand that it means people who are from all genders and all cultures and backgrounds and all classes and abilities and disabilities. To really think about that word 'diversity'.

I moved to Brighton nearly three years ago. I stated that I was moving specifically to live in a city that had its own trans community; to no longer be living in a Devon town as the only "andro in the village". As I see it, any trans persons can chose to live as part of the city populous as a whole and not join in with any of the existing trans groups and trans activism, and thereby not feel a sense of the trans community. Because I have chosen to attend The Clare Project – where I'm really grateful to get regular counselling, because I join in with FTM Brighton meetings from time to time, because I have become a member of the Trans Alliance and sat in on the Council's Trans Scrutiny work, I have a tangible sense of a trans community of persons working for change and acceptance. It's important to me to be normalising the number of trans people there are generally in the nation. Hopefully in our more free city, in our free country, the normalising and acceptance has a ripple out effect globally to the places where trans is just not tolerated.

I'm quite clear that there is not such a thing as the LGBT community – or even an LGB and T community. For me this is just a politically-convenient acronym lumping together a relatively large number of the city's population, who may individually experience significant lesbian, gay, bi and trans communities, but whom I see as having quite separate – although intersecting or interlinking – 'agendas'. Certainly gender and sexuality issues are quite distinctly different.

Personally, I find it easier to be out and about as just another member of the whole, homogeneous and mostly cisgendered society. Although I find it necessary to be out as a trans person – in terms of awareness and appropriate language usage. I don't feel like a 'token' trans person; I'm just another person with their individual interests and foibles, etc. And I see the other so-called trans community members as being quite separate individuals, leading incredibly varied lives: some people being professionals, others unemployed being physically disabled; some people with neuro-behavioural and other learning disabilities; plus students, young people growing up within families, people being parents, and so on. Trans folk too represent the breadth of general society's experience. I would prefer it if we could all see each other more as just another person. Not a gender identity, not a sexuality identity, not a bodily ability identity, just a person.

LUC

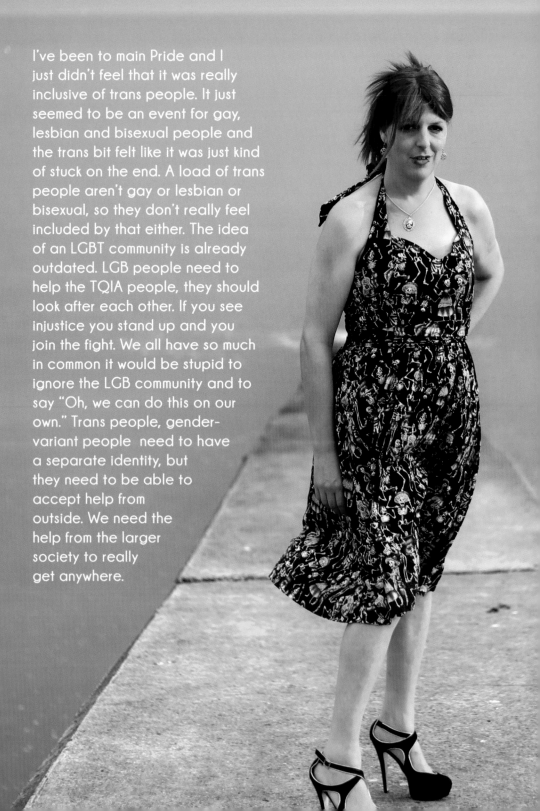

Brighton definitely has a reputation for being trans friendly. One of the reasons I came here was because it had this reputation for being accepting of trans people. I just think people in Brighton are very aware of gender-variance and they've given it the thought that other people around the country haven't. Elsewhere in the country you're more likely to get a reaction out of someone for being obviously trans.

When I first came here, someone invited me to a Trans Pride meeting. I thought it was a brilliant idea and said that I'd give her a hand and see if we can make it happen. And that happened last year, the first one. There was about ten people who were instrumental to making it happen, and in the run up to it we were like, "Ah we'll, we'll be happy if 300 people turn up. That will be amazing". And the last act of the day, there was hardly any room in the New Steine Gardens for people to stand. I think we had a footfall of over 1,500 people. Yeah, I was blown away by how popular it was. Everyone who was gender-variant said that, they felt that this was a Pride for them. I'm really pleased with the atmosphere as well.

I've been to main Pride and I just didn't feel that it was really inclusive of trans people. It just seemed to be an event for gay, lesbian and bisexual people and the trans bit felt like it was just kind of stuck on the end. A load of trans people aren't gay or lesbian or bisexual, so they don't really feel included by that either. The idea of an LGBT community is already outdated. LGB people need to help the TQIA people, they should look after each other. If you see injustice you stand up and you join the fight. We all have so much in common it would be stupid to ignore the LGB community and to say "Oh, we can do this on our own." Trans people, gender-variant people need to have a separate identity, but they need to be able to accept help from outside. We need the help from the larger society to really get anywhere.

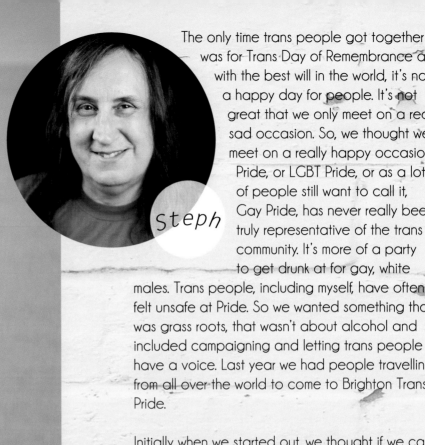

Steph

The only time trans people got together was for Trans Day of Remembrance and, with the best will in the world, it's not a happy day for people. It's not great that we only meet on a really sad occasion. So, we thought we'd meet on a really happy occasion. Pride, or LGBT Pride, or as a lot of people still want to call it, Gay Pride, has never really been truly representative of the trans community. It's more of a party to get drunk at for gay, white males. Trans people, including myself, have often felt unsafe at Pride. So we wanted something that was grass roots, that wasn't about alcohol and included campaigning and letting trans people have a voice. Last year we had people travelling from all over the world to come to Brighton Trans Pride.

Initially when we started out, we thought if we can get fifty people that would be great. To have a footfall of 1,500 people come through the park on a Saturday and over one hundred at the cinema, it was truly amazing. It was a lot of hard work, but it was made worth it by the number of people that came down and the comments that were left. That this is how Pride should be, grass roots people campaigning, not about being a party. There's a hell of a lot of work needs doing to get the trans people to even be treated as equals in this country, and in other countries even further.

Sarah

Stephanie Scott is a Brighton based trans activist, involved in too many good things like being Chair of The Clare Project for over 8 years and one of the Trans Pride organisers.

Ludo

When I first moved here and I wasn't out as trans, I was more identifying kind of as lesbian, I suppose, but more queer really, than anything else. I didn't get a huge sense initially of a trans presence but that was a couple of years ago now. Since identifying myself more overtly as trans, and maybe to do with my study as well, I'm more interested I guess in a queer scene that is more conscious, more inclusive. Brighton is really different from other places in that you do have quite a lot of leeway to be queer and to identify in different ways, but at the same time it's far from perfect. A lot of people might see it as a kind of utopia, but it's far from that I think. I've learnt that.

There is a community that I've noticed more in recent years. There was the big Trans Pride event and a lot of well established, long term projects as well. When I first started to question my gender in a more open way, one of the first things I went to was something called The Clare Project. I think it's inclusive of anyone who wants to go there. But there was maybe one or two other trans guys when I went and so I only went a couple of times. It's an awkward time when you are coming out. You can feel a little bit socially awkward and I certainly felt that way. So going into groups and social situations under the banner of a trans group, I was quite self-conscious. But I made friends and connections and people that I can connect with outside of the groups.

There are certain club nights emerging now. There's something called Fem Rock that is very inclusive, but also quite political as well - quite feminist in an intersectional way. I know people are hearing a lot about intersectionality. It just means being aware of people that are experiencing a marginalised identity, across different things, such as disability, race, sexuality, you know. And how people can be marginalised in a lot of different ways. There's also a group for queer and intersex people of colour as well. This is very open as well, to people that identify under the umbrella. They could be from any particular background as long as they identify in that way. I'm from a mixed background myself and this is a good space. I've become more engaged politically because we are such a small group, the trans community. We've had some amazing forerunners, even thinking in a global sense. And some kind of heroes and heroines that have done some amazing work and have been there right at the forefront of LGBT rights and LGBTQ rights.

Despite having lived here for over six years now, it's only actually been in the last year or so that I've really fallen in love with Brighton. I've always loved this city but it has taken me a while to really find a community here and feel settled. I didn't move here specifically to transition, but I do think it's made it a lot easier, the fact that there is support if you need it, there is a visible and active trans community and more of an awareness of trans issues compared to a lot of other places.

It does have its challenges though, with there being a large visible gay and lesbian community, I found passing took longer here than anywhere else, being read as a masculine woman, particularly when in predominantly L and G spaces was very difficult for a while. I do find Brighton more diverse and relaxed in terms of sexuality and gender identity than a lot of other places but this idea that it's automatically a trans friendly place because of its large gay community is laughable. The majority of the transphobia I've experienced and witnessed has been within LGBT spaces here, I know this isn't the case for everyone and maybe I've just been very unlucky but those are the spaces I feel most uncomfortable. This is one of the many reasons I question the T being part of LGBT. I realise there are a number of ways our communities overlap but as time goes on, my feelings of a separation have become stronger.

I love that there's a lot of diversity in the trans community here as well, I do at times feel in the minority as someone who identifies as a binary transsexual, I haven't yet met many others who share my identity. But it's great that cis-people here are getting more exposure to different trans people's lives, it breaks down people's ideas of what it means to be trans which is a really positive thing. I'm unsure of how out I want to be as a trans person, my identity has changed a lot over time and I'm starting to realise that I'm never really certain about anything. I used to always think I'd be an out and visible trans man, but I also said back then that I'd never take testosterone. I've said a lot of things that are no longer true.

Having Trans Pride last year was amazing, that was around the time I was coming out of my lowest point and was starting to feel comfortable engaging with the trans community here. There was a real sense of pride and inclusion, the opposite of how I'd felt at Brighton Pride in previous years. Meeting people through that and other various trans inclusive groups like Brighton Feminist Collective has made a major difference in my life. Being in those spaces, full of so many supportive, positive people has been one of the best changes in my life over the last year. Having people in your life that are supportive and don't fuck up with pronouns makes such a difference.

Darcy

I came out as trans to my partner in January 2012 and shortly afterwards found the local support group called The Clare Project. Since coming out and living my life as the gender that I feel, I've also found that I'm very drawn to helping other trans women come out and talk about their issues. It's one of the things that I held inside for so long, as a secret, that I was very, very ashamed of and felt that I couldn't talk to anyone about. Just to be able to talk to other women, and girls, who've felt the same way that I did, it's not only helpful for me, but it's helpful for them as well. I get a great deal of joy from it and support.

Brighton is a fantastic place to be honest with you. There's so many things to do, so many groups. I identify as a queer woman. I find a lot of kinship with other people who have varying gender identities and sexual identities and it's just nice.

Rebecca

Ben

I started Brighton University when I was twenty, and I transitioned between the first year and the second year. I really felt like we desperately needed an FTM Brighton, a support group for trans guys in Brighton. I knew there was The Clare Project. I think it had just started around then and I did go to one of the meetings, but it was quite early on and there was only one other trans guy there. So as welcoming as it was, and as lovely as the people there were, I didn't really feel I could relate. There didn't seem to be anyone else I could really talk to about the stuff that I wanted to talk about my transition.

I feel very much like I am part of the trans community now. I'm on the management committee for FTM Brighton and I'm also part of the Trans Alliance, which is a new group that's recently been set up this year. It has representatives from each of the trans related groups in Brighton, so it's a bit like the Power Rangers, the Trans Alliance. I do think we should have a costume, but there we are. So, I'm part of that and I feel like I've connected much better with other people in my situation or with similar journeys over the past couple of years. It's made me feel a lot stronger and a lot more empowered.

I'm working towards giving a very positive view to people that don't have anything to do with the trans community. I'm trying to show that we are normal people. We are just like anyone else, we're human beings. Trans Pride was set up by quite a few people that I know in the trans community in Brighton. It was originally set up by one individual, a trans woman who then couldn't go on to take part in it any more unfortunately because of various personal reasons. But these other people stepped up and put together this amazing event in the summer. It was very community based and a lot of people that went along to it said it was very much how Brighton's main LGBT Pride used to be. It felt very safe. It was much smaller than the usual Pride, and it was fantastic because I got to be there as part of FTM Brighton. So I was on the FTMB stall, but I was also there as Ben the stand up. It was great to have those two points of view and to go round the stalls. It was just a lovely, lovely atmosphere.

In the LGBT community there are things that bring us together and that connect us which are strong. We could use those connections to fight for our rights and fight against discrimination and share understanding and raise awareness. It could be a really powerful bonding of four very separate groups of people. Unfortunately, the reality is that trans people experience of the LGBT community is very varied. There are some LGBT organisations that have a strong trans voice involved in running them. In others, it seems the trans voice is lost in a roomful of other people. Sometimes it's not there at all. I think we're still marginalised, but it has changed a lot in the ten years since I started transitioning.

I've been in Brighton for four years and over the course of that time, now with the Trans Alliance forming and with Trans Pride, there seems to be more of an out and visible trans community starting to form. I'm involved in FTM Brighton and we've been going for three years now. It still feels, in many ways, like quite a fledgling group that's still figuring out what it wants to do. Just being a group that is there for trans-masculine people on a regular basis, that they can just come to, and be amongst their peers, safely, without judgement is a huge thing. People massively underestimate what peer support is, for trans people.

When I first moved here, which was January 2010, there was The Clare Project and that was it. MindOut was alive then but they hadn't done much trans-specific stuff. I went along to The Clare Project and there were no trans guys there and I felt very out of place. So I didn't go back. Then, shortly after that, FTM Brighton started. God knows how I heard about it, but somehow I did and I've been involved in that ever since. First, as just a punter, and then I got involved in the committee. I need to be actively forcing myself into the community to deal with my own stuff. So since then I have made friends and I've dealt with a lot of stuff myself as a result of that, just from the exposure.

Ed

Reuben

I owe Transformers and Allsorts a huge amount for giving me a place where I could figure out how I wanted to be and how I was going to be and how I was going to make myself happy. When you know you don't have to give somebody background on the history of pronouns and the history of the terminology and X, Y, Z.

Something else that I like about Brighton in that sort of same sense is that a lot of things don't need to be said, don't need to be explained. Not necessarily because everybody here is 100% educated on absolutely everything, LGBT or queer related, like. But things just have such less relevance in your place in the city.
I mean when I go back to Essex I have to explain to a lot of people about a lot of different identities. Like beyond my own as well, and also I feel like I need to justify myself a lot more when I'm in Essex or in other places in the country versus Brighton. Because it so diverse, and people come in all different sort of shapes and sizes and identities and expressions that it just doesn't need to said. Things are what they are and they don't need a massive history attached to them.

I work for Allsorts and I run Transformers, which is the group for young trans people, which myself and my colleague Elliot, were asked if we wanted to start. It's the first project of its kind in this city. It's specifically designed for young transgender people and the work that we do with them is awesome.

We go to schools and do training for young people and staff and educational professionals. We worked with The Charlotte Miller art project to produce the Being Human photography book. We produced the Trans Toolkit with the Healthy Schools team, which is basically an instruction manual on how to support trans people.

I totally believe that a safe space is essential. Somewhere we can go and nurture one another and lick our wounds if we're hurt and encourage ourselves and support one another. Where you can go and just be like "This is our space" and put our flag up and do stuff without anyone bothering us, that's essential.

This is a wonderful town. It's got its flaws and it's a hotbed of sleaze, isn't it? Which I quite like. It's a wonderful place to

transition because it's small and there is an actual community here, of people who actually love and respect each other. It is more open-minded on the whole, like I've walked past many a building site and not had any grief off of anyone. I mean that's really sort of stereotypical, but I've pigeon-holed people, expecting them to be a certain way and they haven't been. It's just a good town. I'm proud to call it my home.

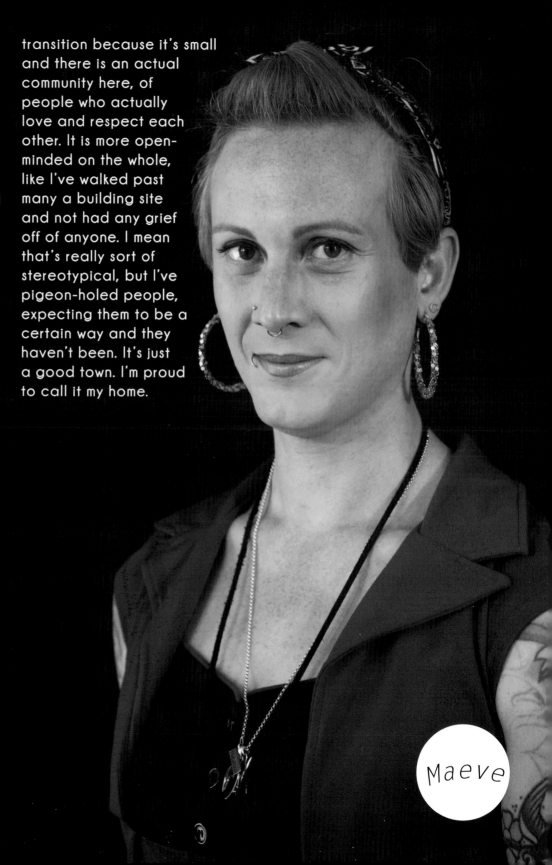

Maeve

Things have kind of exploded. People are finding each other.

Those attending Trans Day of Remembrance has grown in numbers every year. When setting up Trans Pride, I noticed there was prejudice amongst the gay community in the first year we held the event.

The trans scene is emerging now, and Trans Pride will continue to be a positive focal point in the calendar. People are still coming out left, right and centre, regardless of age.

The first year, we had about three months to organise Trans Pride, with about five of us working with loads of support from trans allies. It felt good to celebrate, make connections and share information.

It made my heart swell to see everyone together, demonstrating the need for community and support. We hosted a talented tribe of musicians, comedians, film-makers, artists, who all contributed to an extremely heart-felt Trans Pride, Brighton. It's events like this which will grow in size every year, through word-of-mouth and community spirit.

Fox Fisher is an award winning designer and gender documentor who lives in Hanover with three chickens and a cat. He is a left-handed Scorpio activist, screen-printer, film-maker, creative, dreamer.

The Trans Swimming 'club' was a result of the Trans Alliance, which means on-going weekly swimming sessions, run by volunteers, are subsidised by the local council, every Friday.

It was such an exciting moment when the first session happened. There's so much anxiety that goes with being in a public swimming place. It's a potential mine-field for a trans person. It felt great to have a space without judgement. It's so good for stamina and fitness and for socialising in a place that's not a pub.

It's initiatives like this which make me feel proud to live in this city.

Alice Denny is a parent, friend, (ex) nurse, campaigner for floral dresses, lover of life, poet, Woman.

Chapter Two: I always knew I was different.

Background, childhood, family, parenting, friends, school

Gloria

I grew up near Manchester, with two sisters, in a quite nice area. We weren't wealthy, but we weren't poor. I grew up with all the sixties stuff happening, all the changes in society and the increase in wealth of the country. I felt jealous that my sisters got to wear dresses, they were treated in a different way than I was. The expectations that were placed upon me as a child growing up were far greater, I think, than on my sisters. Although my parents were ambitious for all of us, the level of ambition and the level of drive that was put on me was completely different and I didn't want that. I just wanted to be exactly like my sisters.

From being about four or five years old, my earliest memories were of wondering why I had to wear different clothes; why I wasn't allowed to play with certain toys, why I wasn't allowed to behave in certain ways. and as I grew older, obviously the differences became greater and greater. As my father got older he made a lot of rules for himself and his expectations of others were far higher than I think most people could ever hope to meet. He pushed really hard, particularly for me, to be very successful, and to be ultra-masculine. It was just never going to happen. It caused dreadful problems for me as I went into puberty. It was a nightmare, because I just didn't want to be a man.

I live down here and most of my family still live up north, all centred around Manchester. At the time I used to go up every Bank Holiday. That stopped because I wasn't welcome. It was made very plain to me that I wasn't welcome. I still feel like I've lost my family, that in some way they're gone. I think because of that, it took me longer to settle into my life as a woman, because some of my support network wasn't supporting me. They'd rejected me and it felt very hurtful, devastating. I would sit at home crying, just crying because I couldn't speak to them.

I used to kick and scream a lot when my parents put me into girl's clothes because I have a twin sister; we're not identical, but you know, when parents just have the kind of urge to dress their kids the same. That didn't really work because of us not looking alike. I was much more overweight than her, so it looked almost like a parody. I guess I was obese as a child, I think it kind of covered up my body, so I never really saw my body as gendered. But then, when I started to hit puberty, I realised I was growing breasts and then I just felt really sad. I always knew that I never liked boys but that's what you're meant to do. I always would feel really strongly towards my best friends who were girls. I guess I started to focus on what was wrong with me.

When I came out to my mum and my dad about me wanting to be a boy, by that point friends called me "he" and I was living as a man. I had to almost kind of play up to the usual stereotypical trans person; changing name, you know, going through all the photographic ID stuff and then going to see a GP, hormones, surgery and all that. I think it's more that that made them understand it. My dad, he's really old and he's quite traditional in that way. He just doesn't know much about gender and the medical advancements, so he understood it in the sense that "Oh, right, like you're not just a gay woman, you're a man trapped in a woman's body". I think that's why he's okay with it. And also, having a son in an Asian culture is seen as like so great, it's a real blessing. So, that also helped.

Sabah

Rory

I always knew I was different and I remember crying to my mother when I was about five, six years old, "Why haven't I been born a boy?". I remember my mum comforting me and saying "Don't worry, when I was your age I felt the same", which I find really interesting. So that made me feel "Okay, well it's just normal for girls to feel that way". Then at school for some reason I must have said something as I used to have kids come up to me in the playground saying "Oh, you're the girl that wants to be a boy" and that used to really upset me. Then my teenage years came and I just got more and more odd and different to everyone else.

When I was about fourteen my mum came out as gay and I got quite homophobic at that. I think that's mostly just because it was my mother. Then a couple of years later my sister, who is closest in age to me and we were always pretty close, she came out as being bisexual. And she was in a relationship with a slightly older woman. I remember at that time thinking "Well I can't be gay, like this is silly".

I present as male now, and I'm fine for most people to assume my gender is male. That's how I survive in life and for the most part it works. I've got a female partner so that's what people see.

What was surprising though, I just recently went on holiday, back down to Devon, and I saw my godmother who essentially was my second mother when I was growing up. I went round for dinner with her and her husband and I was really nervous about it because it was the first time I'd seen her since the transition. She knew that I had changed my name because we have very sporadic contact over email. I couldn't remember if I had explained that I was trans and I was undergoing transition. Not only was she like my second mum, she also ran the Sunday School with my mother. I grew up in a single parent Christian household and we were part of this small church community. So I had this double worry also about the Christian aspect of that.

But it was amazing, it was really good to see her. There was no questions asked about my gender identity, about transition, they just accepted me as Rory; she was even calling me he. There was no issue whatsoever and I don't know if that's just because they have that very upper class English politeness where they don't ask or whether it's just generally not an issue. They can see that I'm more comfortable, more happy and a bit more sorted than perhaps I was before.

I remember my mum and dad sitting me down when I was seventeen. I was dripping in eye shadow and like tiny little t-shirts with no sleeves and stuff, and they were like "Are you gay?" And I was like "No," because I didn't feel like I was gay, but I didn't know what it was that I was. And I think Eddie Izzard, my parents thought he was hilarious, so I had that on my side, and I could just say "Well, I'm like Eddie Izzard, you know, I like to dress like this" and they were like "Okay". My mum and dad are just really pleased that I've nailed what's been wrong with me. My mum actually said, "I'm so pleased that you've found what it is. We've been watching you for years. We haven't been able to fathom what the problem's been and we were worried that we were going to lose you," which broke my heart.

They can see that I'm being authentic with what I'm doing. I've heard so many stories about people's parents and families just not supporting them and I think it's absolutely fucked up. I know that I'm lucky because my parents do, but I've also put time in as well, you know, it's not just like "Bam"; it's been a two-way process for a long, long time. The people who are closest to me I think can just see that I'm making the right decision here. I've never been more sure of anything in my life.

UNISEX
SALON

Maeve

E-J

I'm out to all my family. I maintain a very good relationship with them, but I'm very conscious that I don't live in Australia and that makes everything so much easier for me; my past has passed. The truth of the matter is, when I go home I shave off my moustache, because I have such little contact with them that I don't want to spend the two weeks that I'm there with them staring at me inadvertently. Mum and dad still slip up on pronouns all the time; they don't think I'm a man. I have a younger brother, who's my best mate, and he doesn't have a problem with my transgenderism, but he and dad have a sacred bond that is father and son and that is not the same bond that I have with dad; I was his daughter. So, when it comes to real issues of masculinity, I'm ostracised from that intimacy that they share.

My brother doesn't have a problem with my trans status at all, but he doesn't understand why I had to transition. Because when I was a young, radical, queer 'dyke', for want of a better description, I was a raging feminist, I still am. And my brother was brought up by me lecturing him, you know – "Women can do anything. Women are strong." I instilled that feminist ethic that he still holds today. So he didn't understand why I needed a male body to be me and why I needed to do what I needed to do.

I still don't have a lot of the language surrounding having to explain that. I don't have the answers for that. I don't know why I have such a deep-seated problem with my own physicality that I literally had to change gender, because I don't believe in gender binaries, so why on earth did I need to be a man? I don't know, and my brother doesn't know either. But I just have to say to him, "Look how much happier I am" and every time we have this conversation that's where he stops and he's like "Absolutely, there is no denying that, you are happier since you transitioned".

This is my absolute truth, since I have transitioned I am happier, calmer, more focused. I do not suffer from the depression that I was riddled with and that crippled my entire life before transitioning. I have a self-assurance about me that was not there previously. I'm not nearly as angry, even though I've probably got thirty more things to be angry about by being trans. It doesn't manifest in anger, it manifests in action.

I grew up in a high-control religious group, called the Jehovah's Witnesses. I knew that I was different from everybody else about my gender identity when I was about five or six. I also knew that I had to hide this, I couldn't show this secret to anybody. So I kept it to myself and I learnt to compartmentalise my feelings and I learnt to hide who I am from everybody. Yeah, I did it well. I left the religion when I was seventeen because I just couldn't stand lying to everyone. I wanted a life where I could be who I was, who I wanted to be. Then slowly I accepted that I had to transition, but not for want of trying not to. I think I tried every other possible option open to me before I could transition. Even eloping to Las Vegas with a girl that I'd met six weeks before to get married.

Eventually it was the only option left to me and it was the best thing I've ever done. Jehovah's Witnesses preach that if a family member leaves the religion then they should be shunned. They should be cut off as a lesson to them. I wasn't actually shunned completely. My mum and my littlest sister were always really kind to me and fought still to have a relationship with me. My dad, my oldest sister and my little brother never really bothered to speak to me or to have any relationship with me. And then ten years later, when I transitioned that was the final nail in the coffin with everybody, apart from my mum. My dad has banned all contact with me. My mum still keeps in contact, she calls me once every couple of months at the moment. It's shit, but, you know, I can't do nothing about it. I've got to live my life.

Sarah

School anyway was difficult because I'm deaf. I have been since birth and although I had a hearing aid and could hear some things, it didn't help. My teacher had no idea how to educate a deaf child and put me right at the back of the class. So I couldn't hear anybody. I could barely see anybody and I felt completely isolated. I was very unhappy there, it became pretty obvious. I started being bullied by the boys and after about one or two months of it my parents said, "Well, that's enough". They took me out of the school and decided to look for a school for the deaf. The one they decided upon was in Brighton.

I just gravitated towards chatting more with the girls than chatting with the boys. A lot of my friends were girls and that got a bit of teasing from the boys but it wasn't serious. But the crunch came when they asked me to play football with the other boys. I didn't want to play football. I hated football because it was rough, a contact sport. I said to the teachers, "I'm not going to play football", and they said, "Why?". "Because it's a rough sport". "Oh no, you're a sissy," said my PE teacher. So, that sort of cry of sissy has followed me down through the years. When I was adamant I wasn't going to play football they said, "Okay. If you want to be a sissy, play rounders with the girls" and I thought, "Result", because I wanted to do that. Well, really, it was an attempt to humiliate me into conforming. This wasn't done out of the kindness of their hearts.

Next Wednesday the PE teachers came up to me and said, "If you want to play with the girls, you've got to wear girls' PE kit". And they presented me with a pile of girls PE kit complete with infamous green flannel knickers. They made me dress in that in the boys changing room, in front of the other boys, who were told to mock me. Now some of the boys did, some didn't, they were quite embarrassed about the affair. By that time I was so angry with the teachers, that I went ahead. I came out onto the playing field dressed as a girl and the other girls were giggling. But the teachers were saying, "Go on boys, look at the sissy". And the girls thought, "We're not having that", and they closed ranks and stood up for me.

The next week, I avoided the humiliation by changing into these clothes in the boys common room which was empty at the time, then I came out onto the field ready and the teachers plan was foiled. They couldn't really do anything more. That went on for another six weeks, then the headmaster found out. He went utterly nuclear, not so much with me, but with the teachers. So, he called me into his study, and I thought, "Oh I'm in for it". And the first question he said to me, "Is this true you've been playing rounders in girls' kit with the girls?" I said, "Yes". "Have you told your parents?" And I said, "No". He breathed a sigh of relief and said, Okay, forget about this, you're not playing rounders any more. For PE just do some extra study." I was excused PE with the boys for that year. I never told my parents.

Joanna

I was during one of my later medical appointments that I decided to tell people, because I thought, "Well, it's happening now in a more overt way". My sister, at first said, "Well, I can't really see, you know, I can't really equate you". It was when Chaz Bono had come out and so that was a reference at that time. I told her about genderqueer and the variety of different ways that people can express their gender identity. I said I'd send her these videos, which I did, it seemed to be a really good way for people to understand. I am very close to my family and I love them and I didn't think they would reject me and they didn't and I know that's not the case for everyone. So I've been really, really lucky about that.

My mother has been brilliant. Even with things like birthday cards, you know, she's getting male cards now. Not that it always needs to be gendered, but I think for her it was just to show that she's really open with this. She doesn't always get it, but she really is trying. It's only been very recently that I felt confident enough as well to tell other members of the family. I've got a half-brother, that I've recently been back in touch with, and it's meant embracing a whole new side of my family. He's married and he's got a very young daughter. She'd been calling me auntie before that and she said, "Well, now you're Uncle Ludo". That was a fairly recent development.

Ludo

Michelle

My wife knew, and I think we were both complicit in trying to hide it in some way. Early on I felt it was best for my family that they didn't know, especially when children are involved. I actually went back to see my family, my siblings, one last time as male me. I didn't tell them what was going on, but I saw them and I felt like I was dying. I felt like they should see me as I was, because I knew where it was going. And then the next time I saw them I was Michelle. I'd suffered so much depression trying to keep it in, I had to come clean. When I finally told them, I remember they said, "Oh thank god, we thought it was something awful. We thought you were in trouble with the police or something. Or you were ill". Someone gave me some great advice at The Clare Project, because I was so worried about being ostracised or them being angry with me, which was "just tell them how much you love them, and keep telling them you love them and

nothing's changed". I did that, and I think that was the best advice I had, because they know.

My wife wanted me to make a decision, really. She didn't want to hold me back and all-round she's ok, she's a good person. But I think she had some real difficulty with it and I think she felt very hurt. So that side of things has been difficult, pretty much we knew that that was the end of the marriage. That's a huge consequence. I never expected to get married and have to break it up because of this. That was one of the questions that was levelled at me: why would you marry someone when you knew you were a woman or when you knew you were trans? And what I'd say to that is that I went into the marriage knowing there was something about me that was different but thinking that I could make the best of it. It wasn't consciously an act, but it felt like a mask that I had to wear.

Growing up, I did get on really well with my parents and my brother who's a few years younger than me. That all changed when I introduced Rosa to them as my girlfriend when I was around fifteen years old. My mum had an awful reaction, she knew what I was going to say so she just started screaming at me not to say it. She didn't want me to live at home anymore and our relationship hasn't been very good since.

My dad didn't say anything, he kept out of it at the time and we've never spoken about it since. It took my mum around ten years to come to terms with the fact that our relationship wasn't a phase but she's still never referred to Rosa as my girlfriend or partner. I was very close with my brother at one point and he was always supportive but we've drifted apart a lot recently and I haven't seen any of my family in around three years now.

Because of the reaction over Rosa, I was extremely anxious about coming out as trans to them, not helped by the fact that I was so dysphoric prior to medical transition that I was cutting everyone out of my life. They knew something was up, I was speaking to them less and less on the phone, not visiting,

not inviting them here. I tried to convince myself that I'd never have to tell them, that maybe they wouldn't notice, for a while at least. When I started on T they thought I had a cold whenever I spoke to them on the phone, it was ridiculous. Then when I went for surgery, it hit me how far things had gone and how they didn't have a clue about my life or who I was. Knowing my mum wouldn't remain calm enough to have a conversation with me about it, when I got back from surgery I wrote letters to her and my dad. I was really upfront, I told them "I'm a man, I've been on hormones for over a year, I've had surgery, I have a new passport, it's all legal, medical professionals agree with me. I know it will take time to get used to and use the right pronouns but I need you to try, otherwise I can't be in your life" – I just had to give that ultimatum.

I had a better response than I expected, I had a nice e-mail back from my dad, saying it would take a while to get used to having another son but he

just wanted me to be happy. My mum did call me and tell me she still loved me, but won't discuss or acknowledge it. I think there's a possibility that I can build a relationship with my dad, but I can't see that happening with my mum.

I'm at a point now that I've done all I can to try and build bridges, I've invested a lot of time and energy trying to resolve things in the past but realise it's just no longer worth it. I have such an amazing girlfriend and friends here that mean a lot to me and I think my energy and time is better spent elsewhere, on people that do respect me.

Darcy

I don't have a particularly close family, and there's not a lot of us but we see each other from time to time. So really my family is my mum and my sister and maybe a couple of aunts and a handful of cousins. Everyone has been always fine with it and there's been a number of occasions where everyone's been like "Yes, absolutely, we support you. We don't really understand it but we support you".

And then, you know, five years later it's turned out that they had the wrong idea about something, the whole time. They never asked me about it. They never really wanted to talk about what transgender meant, what transsexualism is, why I was doing it, how it affected me as a child. My mum blamed herself, but of course there was nothing she did that made me trans. My dad I don't see often, and I'm not actually sure what he thinks about it. I kept sending him pictures as I transitioned, showing him what I was up to but also so he could see the

changes so I wasn't a shock next time we actually met.

I once went to a support group for families and trans people, and I took my mum along because it was in her town. I thought maybe that'll be a thing to generate some conversation. And when she came out of it she said, "It's funny to think that you've been doing this for three years now". I said, "I've been doing this for ten years now mum, not three." And she was like "Oh yeah." So, I don't know, on the one hand it's great that they've been supportive, but on the other hand I don't know what they think they've been supporting.

Ed

As a parent, the guilt connected to hurting your child is appalling. It's the one thing that's slowed me down in my transition. It's held me back because I wanted my son to get used to it, to understand it. When I told him it was absolutely heart-breaking. It's the hardest conversation I ever had. He still calls me "he", he still calls me "dad" and he doesn't particularly want to talk about it. For me and I think for lots of the trans parents I've spoken to, the fear is being rejected by your children. If you're rejected by your parents that's one thing, if you're rejected by your siblings that's another, but if your children reject you, that's really tough.

I started four years ago and I still consider myself in transition. Maybe I always will, but I know most of that is because of my son. I wanted him to come with me. He's very bright and he gets things, but it is tough for him and I know he doesn't like it – he's told my ex that he struggles with it. She worries about the effect on him but she does support me. She's the best, she's fantastic. I know other trans people who, as parents, have got that ex kind of pouring poison into the child's ears about them as well as the fear and the stigma. I think especially as it's a son, the betrayal of masculinity to him is quite difficult. I have to make it clear that there's nothing wrong with being a man. It's just me. I had a problem with being a man.

Cass

Sam

There are plenty of trans people with kids out there, but the majority of them tend to be trans women who've been married when they were living as male and had children. Their circumstances are often very different; they've usually separated from their children at the time of transition or beforehand, and their relationships with their kids suffer – probably far more than mine has. Fortunately in this country, fortunately for me anyway, children tend to stay with their mother at the time of separation and there was no question about whether my children would stay with me or not.

There have been some implications from some members of my family that my kids would be better off without me, which is really painful and wrong. A good example of that is one of my sisters, when I was discussing feeling suicidal – which I think is a common theme amongst trans people. I said something along the lines of "My kids are better off with a transitioned parent than a dead one". At which point my sister looked at me, and said, "I don't know if that's true" – she said, "I think if you proceed to have surgical treatment for this then you will do your children untold psychological damage – which maybe far worse than that of suicide." So that was pretty confronting and painful to hear, but it's not a bad thing for me to stop and take stock and really think if there is any truth in that – that my children are better off without me than with me transitioning.

Obviously, I came to the conclusion that my kids are far better off with a parent who's alive and able to care for them, than one who isn't. But it did make me think about the psychological impact of surgery and that's quite a significant thing. All my children were breast-fed for example. So we as a family have got to go through a little bit of sort of mourning and grieving and loss about that because there is a part of me that is really attached to them through the modality of breast-feeding. I don't like having breasts and I never have, but I do love the fact that you can grow a baby on the end of one. That's amazing.

So, that's some of the negative stuff, but there's been a lot of positive stuff that having kids has made happen. It's taught me a lot about humanity and people's capacity to adapt; you know, children are immensely adaptable, their brains are still very plastic compared to adult brains. My children were other people's biggest concern when I first started out on this journey, yet they're probably the people in my life who have accepted this most easily and integrated my transition into their life. The kids are really used to saying things like "mum" and "he" in the same sentence without any difficulty, whereas other people really struggle with that. And we'd have conversations from time to time about losing the words 'mum', 'mummy', and 'mother'. But I don't want to impress that upon them. Sometimes I get very dysphoric about it, other times I can cope with it. When we discuss it, we usually come to the conclusion that they can call me whatever they feel comfortable with and they do. They call me a various choice of names, including Sam, Sam-jam, Mum, SJ, all kinds of things, all of which feel quite comfortable.

They do some hilarious things, for example if anybody rings up asking for me in my old name; they'll usually say something quite facetious, like "No, she's dead" or "She doesn't live here any more" or "Don't know who you're talking about". Yeah, so they're pretty useful people to have around. If I'm not feeling strong enough to put people right, they will, they'll certainly do it for me. They go ahead of me sometimes, you know. I'll get a letter that I need to sign and one of them will say, "Oh, I told them you were my dad, is that okay?", stuff like that – so they're doing half the work for me these kids.

Rebecca

We've been together for seventeen years. We recently got engaged, and we are very, very happy. I think before coming out to her, it felt as if there was something missing from the relationship. It's like we didn't quite engage with each other. I've realised it just feels like a very genuine relationship now, whereas before it felt a little bit distant, that she didn't respond to me properly as a person. Now that's she seen who I am and I make sense to her, we're very close.

I live with my two children, and my partner. My children are ten and eleven years old now and they go to the local schools. It's interesting because they both interpret it in different ways. It was a very difficult time, because my partner obviously didn't know what to do or how to do it. Without actually formally sitting down with them and talking about it you can't particularly transition. I put my daughter to bed and I said to

her, "Some people feel as if they're a different gender than their body. Like some girls feel like they're boys and some boys feel like they're girls", I said, "and inside I feel like a woman. I'm going to be changing my gender and my presentation because it's more comfortable for me'. She gave me a big hug and said, "Okay," and that was it. And I said, "Oh, you know, is there anything that you're worried about?" and she said, "I just want to go to sleep". So, that was it. To her then, from that moment I was another woman in the house and she's always treated me that way.

Since then she's been wonderfully supportive. Any little body change, because I'm obviously taking hormones and things, she's been right behind me. I'll never forget we were on the holiday the next summer, and she said, "Wabby" – because she calls me Wabby, not mummy nor daddy because I'm a woman and her daddy. We were on holiday and she said, "Your legs have turned girly" and she got really excited for me and it's just really fantastic. She got it straight away.

My son, on the other hand, was different and when I told him, he bottled it up completely and wouldn't say very much. I knew something was terribly wrong and I had a sense that that would happen anyway. He went through a grieving

process. I remember the next week he was very depressed, he used to take male items of my clothing and what have you; he took my wallet and he said, "Can I have this?" – he was so sweet, because I was obviously changing all my things and I said, "Yeah, of course you can," and he's kept it ever since. One night I found him hugging a pair of my socks. I held him in bed crying all night for his father.

Later on I asked him, "At what point did I change for you? What was the point that I changed, that you felt as if you'd lost a parent?" and he said, "the moment you told me". So it's interesting that the moment I told him was the moment his father died and this woman walked into his life. He's better now. He's well adjusted now. He's got two mums, he's quite happy with that. But yeah, it's just interesting that both my children had very, very different responses.

Rebecca Williams was coercively assigned male at birth and defines herself as a binary-identified woman and bubble blowing queer.

Sabah is fierce, brown, happy and
trans. A feminist at heart, he blogs and
bellows at smashbrown.wordpress.com

Chapter Three: Silence equals death, it really does.

Dysphoria, mental health, stress, coping, escapism, fantasy

Michelle Steele has two children who she loves dearly. She enjoys her allotment, plays drums in a band and works in Brighton writing software.

Michelle

Gender dysphoria ends up with you tearing yourself apart. I felt very uncomfortable in quite a lot of places. I had anxiety, depression and panic attacks in public. I never felt quite right and had paranoid feelings of people looking at me, or I felt ill. I felt like I was sort of dying or ill. This went on for years and years. I tried to cope but I put that down to my own internal struggle with gender. I don't get them now, at all. You really need the doctors behind you with this, so I've actually changed doctors just to find someone who understands. I'm just seeking as much help as I can; I've been referred to Charing Cross, I'm seeing an endocrinologist and two psychologists, so we've been through the whole idea of gender dysphoria. I want to progress with hormones and voice coaching and I'm having electrolysis, so the physical things are really helping my self-esteem. It's very important.

Without those things it's really difficult to feel that this whole thing is going well. I think there's a question over how far you go with everything; I mean I just feel that I'll keep going until my body is matching how I feel inside. I question everything I'm doing to make sure it's the right path for me. I don't listen to too many people because it's my journey. I'm in control of this. Making sure you're in control and you understand what's happening to you is very important. It's also important that people understand I can be a woman, and I can be trans, and it's quite normal.

Sam

One of my psychotherapists said, "Whatever changes you make, if you do it for yourself then you'll be driven and it'll happen". But sometimes I just go under, I can be found sort of quivering in a corner, going "How the fuck did I end up here?". But I think most of us just do our lives, like what arrives in front of you is what you deal with. People who know me well would suggest that I seek stuff, like hardship or battles. I'm not aware of that but maybe that is exactly what I do. I have to say, I do relish the battle. I'm aware that it gives you a boost in self-esteem, when you stand up for yourself; whether you're a trans person fighting for recognition in society or whether you're a parent who's twelve year old is being a little shit.

I didn't do it for a long time, I didn't stand up for myself and it took transitioning to get me to do it as well. I was in a really unfortunate relationship for a long time, getting the crap beaten out of me. I think that's a mark of not coming out actually. Of hiding in the closet, because your self-worth is so low, you're prepared to tolerate almost anything. I stayed in a marriage for much longer than I should have because you don't get divorced in the Catholic church, you just suck it up. But it took a couple of priests to say "It's all right, you know, if you're having the crap beaten out of you, to leave the marriage". I guess that was the first time I stood up for myself and that was quite recent really. It's not over, but I definitely feel like things are getting easier.

I had a funny dream, specifically about transitioning. I was in the Grand Canyon. The Grand Canyon's really different, it's the opposite of a mountain and the exhilaration is in the second half of the journey. Anyway, I was at the bottom. I'd had the easy run down, taking some rest, and getting some cool water. I had the hardest part of the journey ahead and yet somehow I knew I was equipped for it. I've only just recently started taking hormones and surgery will happen in the next year or two. So physically it's going to get harder, but actually in here, emotionally and mentally it's not going to be nearly as hard. I can see that.

Being transgender is still seen as a mental health issue and even though some people will want medical interventions and treatments, certainly not everyone will. A lot of people don't see it as a mental health issue, or even a flaw in themselves. I think that there will be change, and I think it is happening now, but it's a way off. I would like to think there'd be a time when we wouldn't need to have a Trans Day of Remembrance. This is why I like to speak out and to be open, so that I can do my bit as well and be included in that sense.

For me the dysphoria was very much around my body, especially as I went through puberty. It was a sense of a disconnection. I didn't have the words at the age of twelve and thirteen. I just remember feeling a great disconnect from this developing body, especially the chest area. It didn't feel like my body basically. The development with the chest area, was really distressing and became even more so the older I got. Sometimes I would find ways to distract myself from thinking about my body at all. I didn't know about things like binding in my teens, to hide the breast area and to make that flat. So as I got older I would wear layers and things.

I still feel like that, a body dysphoria and it had a knock-on effect as well. It's made sense now of periods of my life when I've experienced depression and really struggled. I always did feel a sense of having to kind of live in my imagination and escape, because of this disconnect with my body. There can be a lot of internalised transphobia and this is something that I still work on; an embarrassment about mental health issues and eating disorders. These things can allow people to feel isolated, and I felt that isolation quite often although I'm trying to shake it off. It's good for people to know they aren't necessarily on their own with these things.

Ludo

Rory

I feel like I've almost wasted ten years of just being a bit lost. I've had lots of depression and anxiety over the years and lots of issues. I've spent a lot of time unemployed because I just didn't know what I was doing with my life and I think if I weren't trans I would have been a bit more on it, I would have studied better at school and I think I would have been a bit more driven with a potential career.

So it's hindered me, the bit prior to transition, and post transition, the first couple of years were really tricky. I was unemployed for a year of it as well and it was really hard getting used to hormones. My life got tipped upside down a little bit, but then I got this great job in the police and things have just worked their way out now. I actually feel like I've got a job that could be a career and I've got prospects. My life has improved through physical transition in that way.

After I accepted myself as a trans woman, after I'd got past that stage, what actually overtook me was an intense feeling of physical dysphoria. I was okay living in that male body, with denial, but as soon as that denial had gone, between me and my pain there was nothing, and it was very, very raw indeed. Raw to the extent that I would cry every night. I know this sounds ridiculous, but I'd put false breasts on so that I would wake up in the morning, and not feel distressed to the point where I couldn't cope. I used to wake up crying, just because I just couldn't stand being in this form for one minute longer. When I came out I was in a place of immense psychological distress. I had a family to maintain, so I decided to self-medicate. I was doing so because otherwise I wouldn't be able to work or even go out of my front door.

Rebecca

Ruth

The great difficulty that we have to overcome is the mental health issue. It's a permanent thing, it's a challenge. I can overcome some prejudice, for instance people who ring me up and think that I'm a male. I have to deal with that regularly and we all do. I'm fortunate because I have the sort of personality that will overcome it face-to-face with most people, but some people are very shy, very embarrassed. Now, there are some people who go through the transgender route because there's no other way they can go. And my belief is that you've got to have a successful and balanced life in the one gender before you've got the ability to carry through the business of changing. Solve your problems then change.

We have to keep a watch out for all the people who might have suicidal tendencies. In transgendered or transvestite groups thirty-six out of every thousand are thought to commit suicide against the national average which I think is four per thousand. It's a huge difference and that obviously has it's roots in mental difficultly, which has to be addressed by the mental health specialists. That's the overall picture that should be addressed by all of us, because we ourselves have a responsibility to improve this.

Maeve

I'd never made an actual suicide attempt, but I've been irresponsible. There've been days when I've just thought like, "I'll have another one of them, maybe I won't wake up. It'll be all right". I never cut myself because I was always really stubbornly proud but there are ways of hurting yourself that look okay. It's kept me indoors. There was a week when I was just like "I can't go out, like. I'm not sick, but I'm calling in sick. I can't do it. I can't be out the house, I can't see anyone, I can't perform any tasks". It was awful. Sometimes you're just like "Buck up, this'll be fine" and sometimes you just think "No, sod it, I'm closing the curtains. I'm just going to wait until this passes".

So I did, I just went to ground for a week. I watched telly, or played like crap computer games and ate biscuits and waited. Then towards the end of the week the clouds just rolled off and I was like "Ah". I felt well better after that. That was a real turning point for me. Just for giving myself the time. And I came out of that just feeling loads stronger. That's when I really started to think "Right, let's crack on now, let's get into the world".

I had a lot of counselling and help with the anxiety problems, because obviously having problems like that while you're studying for your finals is not helpful. Later it forced me into being a workaholic, to keep it all locked down. Because it meant I wasn't concentrating on anything but work. I didn't have to deal with issues in my private life. But even then it would bubble to the surface every so often. I suffered from anxiety issues for quite a protracted period of time and I had treatment for that; beta-blockers, to deal with the anxiety, but not to deal with it.

People weren't dealing with gender dysphoria then and I became a workaholic; not a bad thing because it did mean I moved up the ladder very quickly. It meant that when I started my consultancy business, I was in demand. I was still trying to conform, so I had several girlfriends. In the early nineties I lived with somebody for nearly nine years. So I did my best to conform, but the pressures from my gender dysphoria would always take me back to being on my own: to be me in private, so that I could dress the way I wanted to, behave the way I wanted to, in private.

Gloria

Joanna

Deaf and trans, Joanna Rowland-Stuart has resided in Brighton since 1959. She is involved with Brighton's LGBT Community Safety Forum and is Trans Liaison for Regard, a charity for LGBT people with disabilities.

Halfway through the first year of university, I realised, although I had decent A-Levels, that I was struggling. It didn't help that I had no support to help me with my communication as a deaf person. I wanted to explore what I'd discovered in myself when I was at grammar school, about being female, but I was terrified of being expelled from university and disappointing my parents. So I went quite the other way. I grew a beard, a moustache, I started wearing very male clothes and smoking a pipe, instead of cigarettes. It was completely sort of overcompensating and I joined the Christian Union and started evangelising. Eventually I went to the Dean and said, "I can't cope" and I seriously, at one point, considered ending my own life. I didn't want to disappoint my parents. It sounds stupid, but I was also dreadfully confused over who I was.

After I graduated my friends were basically trying to get me married off. My parents were puzzled that I didn't have a girlfriend. It was difficult and how could I explain to them? It was very hard. I met a girl, and hormones took over and we were married. I mean it was mental, absolutely mental, but then you have to conform. My marriage ended and I moved back to Brighton and lived in a one bedroom flat on benefits.

When I went to the Job Centre they turned round to me and said, "Don't bother signing on any more. You're obviously not going to be employed, because you're deaf." It was so soul destroying and I found myself in my flat, crying and thinking "What do I do? Maybe I should just drive my car off Beachy Head", which I was seriously thinking of doing. Then I thought, "No, that's not fair to my children", I had two – and "it's not fair to my parents". I thought, "No, that's a coward's way out". I can carry on as I am, a failure as a man, that's how I thought of myself, or I can just try and explore who I want to be.

We have to put ourselves out there, there's no other way. As the old Act Up slogan says, 'Silence equals death', and for us it really does. Because how many of our brothers kill themselves because they never get to a point of realising that it's possible to transition? Living with the dysphoria is just unbearable. The only way that we can deal with that is to be visible and out as trans men ourselves: I have chosen to be very visible as a trans man. I was reflecting on this because I was really aware that before I transitioned, there was this crushing sense of shame. I could have never imagined that I would be as out as I am now because I was just wracked by shame.

I think I really have to pay tribute to good friends that I met through FTM London, and latterly FTM Brighton. And also another organisation called Trans Bare All; a couple of guys who run retreats for trans men. They focus specifically on issues of body image and feeling comfortable with your body. And parts of the retreat are often done naked. That can be a really challenging thing, but that process really enabled me to throw off some of that shame and come to a place of being proud of being trans. So that was really important for me.

Cass

Nick

I remember I had lots of fantasies, and they weren't sexual. They were just fantasies. If I watched a sci-fi film, in my fantasy dream, there would be a spaceship come along and they would realise I was really a girl. And they would take me away and I'd become a girl by magic, because their spaceship was magic. It always involved someone else coming in, recognising me for who I was and transforming me to the person I should be. I think that's very common in a lot of trans people. A lot of trans friends of mine have had those same fantasies when they were children.

This gay woman I work with, she was amazing and we just got drunk one night and we were comparing notes on identifying with the wrong person in a movie for your gender. And I was saying how I always wanted to be the Bond girl. But everyone thought I liked James Bond movies because I wanted to be James Bond. It was actually because I liked the Bond girls. Not because I fancied them, but because I wanted to be one. I fantasised about being Princess Leia, you know, especially in some of her outfits in the last film.

Luc

One of my greatest challenges has been the lack of awareness in society of the various conditions that I have lived with, resulting in the fact that I didn't receive diagnoses of these until I was in my late forties or early fifties. It was another trans male who suggested some four years back that I might be on the autism spectrum and told me that there's actually a twenty percent higher incidence amongst trans people of having Asperger Syndrome.

In Brighton, unusually, there is an adult support group, and I joined this and also made a request to have the neuro-behavioural clinic's assessment and received a diagnosis of having Asperger's last summer, at age fifty-four. It's been a huge revelation to me and a relief, because it's answered a lot of problem issues and queries that I had around my challenges of relating to people. This effectively stopped me having a degree, having a career and having partnerships. But it's also given me another label to be political about.

I don't feel as though the Aspie side of me has been compromised by or has compromised my trans identity at all, perhaps it's even enhanced it. Aspies have an intense need for honesty, for a sense of integrity, so I am unable to live a lie, whether that means getting in trouble for what I am saying, for how I behave, or for having to move on from activities and people dynamics. I have a bipolar disorder level II diagnosis from 2004, when I made a first suicide attempt and was hospitalised in a psychiatric unit, but my supposed unipolar depression started when puberty set in at eleven. In 2009 I received a diagnosis of fibromyalgia, although I had probably lived with that since I was kindergarten age.

Fortunately, following recovery from a serious overdose in 2007 when I literally 'woke up' to knowing that I needed to transition to be the androgyne person I was, the art therapist from the same hospital unit (to whom I was re-referred for post-crisis therapy), knew about the Gender Identity Clinic in the next door building. My GP did not mention it – and I don't think my psychiatrist even knew of it at that time. But, once I was referred to a GIC consultant psychiatrist and diagnosed with gender dysphoria, that became the sole access to mental health treatment; I was very lucky in that I received four years of ongoing gender counselling there from a therapist who was able to recognise the validity of my non-binary gender identity. But art therapy for the invisible disabilities in my life in general was 'off'.

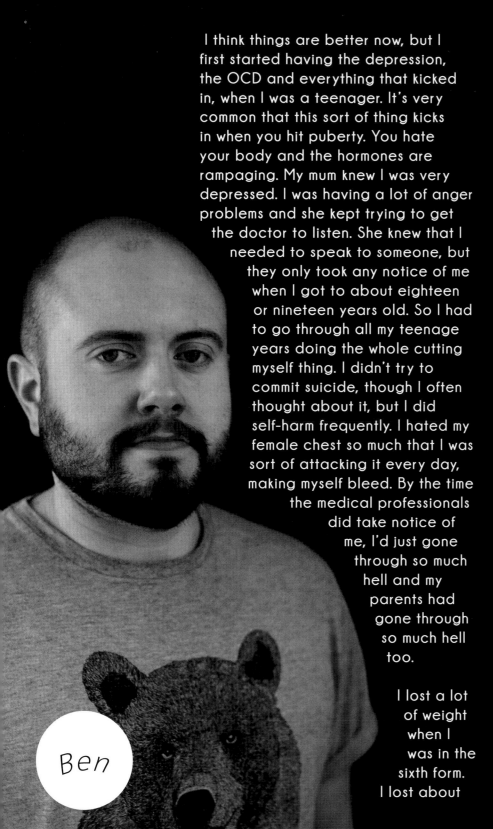

Ben

I think things are better now, but I first started having the depression, the OCD and everything that kicked in, when I was a teenager. It's very common that this sort of thing kicks in when you hit puberty. You hate your body and the hormones are rampaging. My mum knew I was very depressed. I was having a lot of anger problems and she kept trying to get the doctor to listen. She knew that I needed to speak to someone, but they only took any notice of me when I got to about eighteen or nineteen years old. So I had to go through all my teenage years doing the whole cutting myself thing. I didn't try to commit suicide, though I often thought about it, but I did self-harm frequently. I hated my female chest so much that I was sort of attacking it every day, making myself bleed. By the time the medical professionals did take notice of me, I'd just gone through so much hell and my parents had gone through so much hell too.

I lost a lot of weight when I was in the sixth form. I lost about five stone, and when I went to college I put it all back on, plus more, in a matter of about three or four months. Then one day at college, I had a breakdown in the middle of one of the classes. We were doing photography and I locked myself in the darkroom and just completely broke down. I didn't really know why – I was just so unhappy. The tutor told me to go to the counsellor there and I formed a really good close bond with her. I kept saying "I hate my chest, I just want my chest reduced", and she said, "Well are you sure that's what you want?" and I was like "Yeah, that's what I want". But then she started bringing up things about "Do you want to be a guy, have you ever thought about being a guy?". She was the one that made me realise it was possible.

I'm very, very lucky in that my parents are supportive, particularly my mum. I'm very close to her. I think I always thought, "Oh, once everything's finished I'll have a much better life and I'll be much happier". Well as things have gone on, I've realised that it isn't a magic key. Just because you transition, you're not suddenly going to be become some extremely happy individual. I think it's part of my nature to be very susceptible to bouts of severe depression, and to have the OCD, though I'm hoping once the surgery is finished that that will get better. I don't think either of the things will ever be cured, but it will get a lot better.

Ed

I can say categorically that my mental health was terrible before I transitioned; absolutely terrible. I'd been in a psychiatric hospital three times within five years before I started transitioning. I'd dropped out of university. I'd gained massive amounts of weight and I barely left my house. My life had pretty much ground to a halt and I didn't know why. I'd seen lots of mental health services, I'd seen all kinds of different doctors and psychologists and support groups, I'd been on different medications – I just felt like there was this massive pain that I couldn't find and couldn't bandage. I just felt like I was screaming all the time and I didn't know why. I just wanted everything to stop. I just wanted the pain of everything to go away. I wanted to be somewhere really, really quiet, out of my body, and

because I couldn't articulate it and could only talk about anxiety and unhappiness and stress, the health services weren't able to really help me all that much.

It wasn't until I realised that I was trans that I could refocus everything in my life and see it through a trans lens. Then it made more sense. I could see then that there were certain things that were never going to change. I probably was never going to have the body that I felt I should have. I was never going to be born a little boy and grow up and have the experiences as a child and as a teenager that I expected to go through and at the same time I couldn't erase the experiences that I had gone through. So, mental health services could only do so much.

I can remember being on a train and feeling just a bit overwhelmed by "This is going to be the rest of my life," and that I was going to be on hormones and have to have surgery. I was always going to be a bit of a patchwork doll of bits and pieces to make my body feel bearable. And I thought, "god, you know, I could give this three years and if it's awful I'll just kill myself". It wasn't like I was depressed. What I was saying to myself was, "This is your only choice, there is no other choice". And that was a relief. I didn't have to spend my life

as some kind of horrible monster, which is what I felt like I might be.

Discovering MindOut was a life-changing event. I came across them just as they were about to start running their first trans mental health support group, and it was perfect; exactly what I needed. It was a place where I could go and chat about mental health stuff without worrying about outing myself as trans and where I could chat about trans stuff in a mental health context. Sometimes it's just "God, is there anybody else who thinks this sucks?"

MindOut were really, really good. I went to their trans support group for several months and then just carried on going to their general group where I was out as trans. It would have been too hard to not be out where you have to talk about mental health stuff and, that weekly, somebody asking you, "How are you doing this week?" It made a huge difference. I really don't know why that worked whilst all the counsellors and psychologists that I've seen have made less of an impact. Maybe it's because of where I was in my life, as well, in other words I was really ready to just be more stable. I'm a trustee with them now, so obviously I'm biased, but yeah, I think they're awesome.

I've always known about this ache in me, yearning. But when I was younger there wasn't a common vernacular of transgender and I didn't think that what I secretly wanted was in anyway possible so I found distractions. I realised a long while ago really that my nursing was a female distraction. It enabled me to show my female side and it happened accidentally. Having a family was an accident and I loved that. It helped me distract myself with the feminine side I think. Then when that started to come to an end that ache became worse and worse. It got so bad that I was really desperate – Samaritans desperate – but luckily I came upon the LGBT switchboard. I then found The Clare Project and then I found Brighton.

After about a year of travelling over once or twice a week, I decided to try to move here for a while in order to more easily and more quickly get through with what I then understood was transition. So I just had what I thought were almost sordid fantasies about being a woman. At the time I had this big cyst in my neck and I used to have to go into the tunnel to be scanned and I used to dream of just going into the tunnel and coming out as Alice at the other end.

I used to wish I was gay. I used to be quite envious of gay men and androgynous men as well. I mean David Bowie was a little hint, but it wasn't quite me. I kind of knew it wasn't me to be what people used to call effeminate. I wanted to feel it inside more than outside. I just wanted to be me. I'm really happy being me now. This is okay, with all my warts and faults and things that I have to carry on worrying about, just like all other women I suppose. This is how I was meant to be. I really actually think that I couldn't have come out when I was younger. I'd have been wired up to the mains and zapped – that is what would have happened.

Alice

Darcy

My dysphoria got worse and worse over the years, I always had a certain level of physical dysphoria, for as long as I can remember, but my social dysphoria reached its peak a few years ago. My mental health suffered greatly during that time and my reaction to that was to shut myself off from the world. I didn't access any support groups despite knowing they were there, I'm not sure why that was and how different things might of been if I had. I was so absorbed in my issues at the time that I guess partly I felt uncomfortable accessing trans spaces, the whole comparison thing, I didn't want to see people further along in transition than me. It's a horrible thing to say but yeah, I didn't want to feel any worse. But I didn't cope with things very well by myself and on reflection would have done things very differently, but when you're in that place, nothing you do is very logical.

It's been interesting for me to see how much of my anxiety and depression and stress was down to my gender dysphoria. Prior to transition, I was so scared that none of that would change, but that couldn't be further from the truth. Starting treatment has been the most beneficial thing for me in terms of my physical and mental health and for the first time I've felt like I'm actually living my life and really want to be here. The medical side of transition is so important and necessary for so many people, without it I wouldn't be here basically.

I kept having panic attacks before I transitioned and now I don't. It took me 10 years to finally go ahead with my medical transition. I felt so inherently disconnected from the body that I was in. I had so much self-loathing. I hated every cell in my body, and that was really hard to live with. So many things gave me huge anxiety. I realise now that people shouldn't feel like that, and life is meant to be enjoyed. Some people very close to me have bailed out of life because of social pressure, fears, depression.

Some people confess that they would really love to transition but because they didn't do it before 'the wrong puberty' and the setting of their bone structure, they just felt like it was too difficult to go down the path of transition. It's so sad that we have to police gender in such a way that in order to transition successfully you have to look a way that people would never even guess, or know about your history.

I would never want to erase my past, my history. For me it's been a journey of self-love and self-definition. Alignment with self. I love the terms genderqueer and androgynous. Gender is incredibly fluid.

FOX

Sarah Savage is a trans woman who moved to Brighton from Jersey. She's an activist, Trans Pride organiser, children's author and speaker who is obsessed with the internet, motor racing and cats.

Chapter Four: We're all such beautiful people. It would be a shame to hide us.

Coming out, self acceptance, bravery, visibility, style

I love looking male. I love having a beard. It's kind of weird though; if I ever shave it off, I feel like Samson. I'm not me without it, and I don't feel right – plus I look about seventeen. If I ever get down, that is something I have to think about: the times when I was five or six and drawing a moustache on, or drawing a beard on and going "Oh, this is never going to happen". I feel much more comfortable now. I don't think it's particularly about being a guy, or being a woman (if it was the other way round), it's just that I feel much more comfortable being in the body that I always should have been born in.

I've only felt more comfortable being open about being trans since I've almost finished all the surgery. I've been a lot more comfortable with my body and I've lost five stone this year, so that has helped a lot. Obviously the curves that were there have gone, although they do reduce down when you start on the testosterone. Your body structure changes slightly, muscle structure, etc. I don't go round telling people I'm trans. Obviously if it comes up, I will say, although I still find it very difficult with dates because I don't tell people unless it starts going somewhere. I feel that I'm strong enough in my male identity now to be open about my past. Whereas whilst I was going through it all, I was so self-conscious that I just did not want people to know. I'm fine about it now I look completely like a male and no-one would guess.

Ben is an actor, stand up and general funny beardy bloke. A Brighton boy via parental heritage, he is also on the management committee for FTMBrighton.

Ben

Cass

I don't want to be a stereotype. I promised myself that. I still wear Dr Martens boots but I wear them with different kinds of top. All the women I've known and loved as friends have been the kinds of women who'll wear Dr Martens boots and an old jumper if they're cleaning out the garden. And if they're going to a party, they'll wear a dress. One of the nice things about becoming a woman is there's a freedom in terms of the wardrobe you can choose from. It isn't about wearing a skirt either. It did feel at times, when skirts were forbidden that the skirts held such power because they were so forbidden. That it was like the biggest rebellion.

The first time you go out of the house in a skirt, it's like "Oh my god. The world's going to explode." I turned all the lights out in my flat, and I was watching out of my window, to make sure no near neighbours were

walking past or getting in their car. It was quite late at night, my street was quiet, and it was dark. But I was in terror that I'd meet someone, one of my neighbours and of what they might think. It took me about an hour just to get out the front door and walk to my car and drive round Brighton in a dress and then come home again. And I was shaking like a leaf. It feels so ridiculous now, that I don't care what my neighbours think, it's the last thing I worry about.

That's the fear and that's the obsession with passing: being called "mate" by the bus or taxi driver or actual fear of those thugs seeing you and seeing something that they don't like and beating you up for it. I think it comes back to the stereotypes. When I was early in my transition, when I was more masculine, if I'd been genderqueer and just had a shaved head and I hadn't made

a big effort to be feminine, didn't wear a wig, my life would have been unbearable. If I made a big effort and was very feminine, then people would just leave me be or wouldn't notice me.

Passing is about survival more than anything else, it really is about survival. I think it's gone well, it's not as hard as I imagined it would be. I think fear of the whole process is so huge and so deep-seated. I will never be the woman I would love to be because I'm too tall and I've got big hands. But when I get on the bus and I'm called 'love' by the bus driver, when I get called 'darling' or 'sweetheart', it's terribly sexist, but it's great confirmation. And when I used to complain about feeling like my body didn't work in the clothes I wanted to wear, all my women friends were "Well, welcome to womanhood, honey."

Michelle

I'd lived in Brighton for twenty years, but in a relationship and I'd eventually married and had children. Then last year I found myself questioning what was going on in my head. I'd met some cross-dressing people and some people that were ambiguous and androgynous and things. I was very pro androgyny, and I was very pro feminism, and very pro queer, and lots of things that weren't typically heterosexual male-orientated things. Yet I couldn't grasp my sexuality because I didn't know if I was gay or not. I didn't think I was, so the whole thing was very puzzling in my mind.

I'd never really understood transgender and never really thought I would be transgender but I started feeling very much like I needed to wake up. I looked up at the sky, and I looked at the stars, and said, "What am I? Someone tell me." And at that moment I saw a shooting star go past, incredible. I don't know how much of that was subconsciously that I wanted to do something. People talk about the choice, and there isn't a definite moment of me choosing, there was just a waking up.

My first avenue was The Clare Project in Brighton. I felt that I needed to talk to someone, and find someone like me just to get my head around it. But I was very wary about going because I didn't want to get influenced in any way. I wanted it to be my journey and to work out myself exactly what's going on. It was such a huge thing to do and I was in this limbo of deciding whether to keep on trying to repress for other people's supposed benefit or to be real and true to myself, and for my family to find out exactly who I was. I think my relationships with people now are a bit better. I feel much more true to people and much more interested in other people. So that's good. I feel I've got better bonds with some of my closer relatives, and that's purely because I feel I'm being myself to them. I don't have to lie, so that's great. I think that's really important for all of us, to actually have some involvement in changing people's minds and perspectives, and their seeing how important it is for everyone that we are ourselves, and we're diverse and we're creative and that we contribute. We're all such beautiful people. It would be a shame to hide us.

I sort of experimented with being a drag king. I met my partner for several years and with her got involved in the Sussex University Gender Society. I ended up forming a drag king troupe, not to do with the university at all but it came out of it somehow. It was through this drag kinging that I started to explore my gender much more because we would be dressing up in drag and I would be putting on a fake moustache. I became Rory Raven, the drag king and all my friends started calling me Rory and I wanted everyone to call me 'he' now too and so I started really exploring it that way.

Eventually my partner at the time, for my birthday, gave me a binder to help with the drag kinging. Once I got it on, finally when I managed to squeeze myself into it, I loved it. I just loved the fact that suddenly the chest had disappeared. Not that I had a massive chest in the first place but just that flatness was really wonderful. It was like "What's the difference between Rory Raven on stage and Rory in real life?" And it was just the fake moustache really. So I gave up the drag kinging and took off the fake moustache and just started living as Rory. It was weird that I had been working for a trans charity for a couple of years before I actually started really figuring out that maybe I was trans. Maybe that's why I got particularly interested in that job. It wasn't just because it was a job that was vaguely to do with LGBT. There was something else going on and it's just developed on from then.

Rory

I'd been dressing in girl's clothes since it first occurred to me. I was very young, and as I got older I thought if I'm going to have some fun, I'm going to have to be myself. So I'm going to have to be slightly open about being transgender. When I went to university it knocked my confidence hugely and I stopped, for a good few years, even trying to express that side of myself.

Then a partner and I got together and I just pushed it all back into the closet. When we moved down here and we lived together, I wasn't free to do that around her, and I didn't do it. I had expressed that quite freely to myself and around friends in my teens. Then I pushed it back inside in my early twenties when I started the relationship with her; without that being a factor in my life. To get that back I would then have to bring it up with her and introduce it as something new and that was really intimidating. But then every time she was out of the house, because I worked shifts I'd often have the morning and afternoon to myself, and I'd just be in frocks around the house and thinking that it was a sexual thing or a fetish thing. Because I used to get like a real sort of sexual rush out of it. Then eventually over the years I've realised that I felt that way because that's actually just me being me and that sort of rush of sexuality wasn't an end in itself, or a fetishistic thing, it was just me thinking "Oh god, I actually feel good."

Maeve Devine left the Northwest in 1999 and drifted to Brighton. She's been a forklift truck driver and a bar maid. Currently, she leads the Transformers work for Allsorts and works as a barber.

Maeve

Gloria

I dressed in private and occasionally in public, but it had to be a good excuse; a reasonable opportunity, like a fancy dress party. When I was a student at sixth form college, we used to do a rag week, and there was a parade around the town, with bucket shaking. And I always dressed as a tart, because it was my opportunity to be female and feminine.

I used to parade around the town. I used to do the rag week, drama shows and stuff like that, but I would always take female roles. So it was excuses like that to dress in public, but I would dress in private anyway, whenever I could.

The lives and experiences of trans people in some respects are no different from anybody else's. We have to eat, work, live. We like entertainment, reading, the TV, everything that anybody else in society would want to be involved with. But I would want them to think that this time in the world, the early twenty-first century was a major point in trans history. That people are widely accepted as being human beings, and not pigeon-holed because of their gender, or their chosen gender. That actually it's about people, it's about humanity and that this time in history is a major point for realising that.

I did explore a lot, I wasn't afraid of doing that. But it was the coming out and the "What's wrong with you? What will my parents say?" and friends at school and that kind of thing – that was really scary. I was too invisible to get bullied and I was at the right level of smart not to get teased for it. So, a lot of it was just internal hatred I suppose. It was really hard because coming from a South-Asian culture, you just don't get people like me.

It's quite straight-forward what your life should be if you're a girl, and another way if you're a boy. I think it's made people think a lot about gender. It's made people question the usual stereotypes of masculinity and femininity. It was something that was so hidden before. You were told to keep it hidden. People wanted to erase trans people into binary identities, just move from one to another, just do it as fast as you can, pretend it never happened. A lot of people are thinking about gender. I think people realise that it doesn't mean you want to wear different clothes or go for surgery or start hormonal treatment. It's more personal. It's really lovely.

Sabah

Sarah

I knew that I couldn't transition in Jersey: I was absolutely sure about that, because Jersey is nine miles by five. It's tiny and I was aware of other trans people over there. I'd never met them, but my friends knew of them and they were always known as – excuse my language – "that tranny". I didn't want to be that person. I was searching for some way to get to the UK and I did it from meeting people on the internet and chatting to them. I met someone in South Wales and she said, "Come and live with me, I'll help you transition". So I sold, got rid of everything, jumped in my car, went to South Wales, and that didn't work out. So, I jumped back in my car and went back to Jersey.

Then I was living in my car on the beach; because I'd given up everything I had nowhere to live. So I spent two months in Jersey before I got the money together to get the boat fare back. It was kind of a convoluted story about how I came to the UK. I wear a wig, I haven't had laser hair removal on my beard yet. Getting a job and having to shave every day and having to put make up on every day, it takes a lot out of your skin. It takes a lot out of you physically as well. If I know that I look rough in front of someone that I don't know, then I'm more likely to not say anything; not open my mouth. I'm more likely to not make eye contact, to revert back to how I used to be. A quiet person who just kept to myself. And that's not how I naturally interacted. When I've got a face on and I'm freshly shaven, I just feel so much better about myself. I'm just so much more confident.

I knew I was trans forever, but it was still illegal to be gay when I was growing up, let alone there being words for and ways to be trans. There used to be this tree in the park of the little town I grew up in where queer kids used to hang and kill themselves, always on the same branch. So, the word 'trans' just didn't exist and there was no social support for it. There was no 'T' in LGBT, nothing like that. I actually started up the first queer group at our university in 1990. We began using queer terminology in the early nineties and that was giving us some more freedom and that's where I sat with being trans. Australia was more isolated, obviously, because back then it wasn't in the European loop or the American loop of trans awareness, even though it is really, in some ways, very, very forward thinking in some parts of the country. But the early nineties, it was still just lesbian and gay.

So I had to work within those parameters; carving an identity out as queer, not as lesbian, and identifying as an androgynous queer and saying that I was not a lesbian, but not having the words for being trans. So, my partner knew, my friends knew, everyone knew, but I really thought there was no hope in hell of me being able to transition. I saw no physical way of it happening, without losing absolutely everything including my family

and my job. And so it took until I physically crashed and burned and had a break down and lost my partner and literally couldn't go on. There was nothing I could do about it, I was out of control and hysterical at the confusion of it all and knew no other trans people and couldn't see my path ahead. But I wasn't going to be alive if I didn't transition when I did. I'd put it off for too long anyway. And living with that fear and trepidation and self-loathing is so devastatingly exhausting.

You're going to get a much better citizen in broader society out of me if you let me transition happily and just get on with living my life without being wracked with anxiety and lost inside my own dysphoria. Those months prior to my transition were so ghastly I am still deeply hesitant to let myself even think about it. As soon as I had my first shot of testosterone I was a new man; back on track to live the rest of my life as me. I had a lot of making up to do, a lot of getting back on my feet, but from the moment I took T I was waking up every morning looking for whiskers and singing Barry Manilow songs to test if my voice was breaking and basically going through puberty as an adult with all the bouncy excitement of a teenage boy. I was starting afresh and felt alive and like the world was out there just waiting for me to explore.

E - J

I did identify in quite a private way, throughout my twenties and thirties, gravitated towards a queer lesbian identity but I never really had a big coming out or anything like that. It was more just a private thing so people could presume what they wanted really. But I always pretty much presented in an androgynous way: usually short hair, apart from a period in my teens when I was into the heavy metal and stuff like that.

I was quite cut off actually from my gender identity, in a sense, because I couldn't easily access information. So when I got into my late twenties and thirties, getting online obviously transformed things for me. I was able to discover a lot more, and I went on to do my degree and my MA in Fine Art and one of the things I became really interested in exploring in different types of ways was gender. That was always a big interest. Actually even as a child I was always interested in comics and I would always draw cartoon figures and things like that. And very often, if not always, I would draw male figures so there was almost living out this little private cartoon world of being a boy, and giving the character a name.

So, I lived in my head quite a lot and that was a good escape I suppose. It was slow, the whole issue of coming out for me.

Ludo

People have got to recognise that there are those who are living in a gender mixture, rather than either male or female decidedly. So, it's better that people who say, "Well, I wonder if that's a man, or I wonder if that's a woman" are not being too bothered about it. Because I'm not bothered and if I'm not bothered why should they bother? I don't generally go around saying "Look here, I was a man," or something. I say "Well, you know, you probably realise I'm transgendered" and they say "Yeah, we thought so" and that's as far as it needs to go.

We've got public opinion to change and that basically is only done by example.. It can be done by us being out there in front of people, not in any way pretending to be something we're not. I live as a woman, I get treated as a woman, I'm happy as a woman. My friends in every way respect me as a woman: but I'm still out there. People still see me, and some people say, "Well, that's not a woman". I don't want them to have a bad opinion of somebody they think is not a woman. I want them to have a good opinion. I don't mind that they think I'm not a woman, I mind that they think bad of me and that's the important differentiation. I don't want to have to pass in every single case, it's not possible. You can't fool all the people all of the time, but you can make a good impression on all of the people all of the time and that's the important part of it and, if we all do that, then society comes round and says "These people are nice people".

81 years old, Ruth Rose engages on behalf of older people. Public speaker and broadcaster. Former RAF Flying Officer. Transition after retiring. All-year sea swimmer.

Ruth

Luc Raesmith, 'TGQI' second-puberty saga-age person with difference-abilities: activist, blogger, creative recycling artist, mobile photographer, plus...

Luc

When she was three years old, my niece told me "Luey, I don't know if you are a man or a lady". That was a turning point for me aged forty-four; I began to verbalise my identify as androgyne, meaning, for me, both male and female – and yet neither. Before that I hadn't had an absolute realisation in my mind until I was forty years old, when my head was shaved for charity. I saw this 'neutral-looking' bonce of mine and thought "This demonstrates my androgyny." There were plenty of clues beforehand, up to that point, but there was no language about that in society. 'Androgynous' described more often how lesbians were dressing in the seventies and eighties. Now, in my mid-fifties, I identify as transgenderqueer and use less the title androgyne – though I'll say 'andro' of myself to be the equivalent of 'guy' or 'gal'. Occasionally I'll even say I'm transintersexual meaning that my identity is electively hermaphroditic. Because of the lack of language in the last century, I (and others) couldn't register the concepts and since then I have been creating my own language, including alternatives like 'sysbro' and 'dortersun' and 'aren'tunkle'.

I think one of the things that I've done throughout my life to express my difference, wc dressing unusually. Ironically when experimenting as a teenager with my first clothin 'allowance' going down to a gender-neutral changing room in the Oxfam shop, I was often accused of being tarty or whoreish; similarly when I cut my hair. It was so ironic, because I really was this closet asexual. It was ho I played with my fundamento identity, but without having the conscious awareness that that was what I was doing. Now I've got more of a masculine wardrobe, but it's a dual – and enormous – wardrobe because I've worked at Oxfam for a long time and also at Shabitat's Shabby Chic department in this city. It's also linked in wi being an artist and I feel lik my wardrobe is my palette.

I've trained in colour theraƥ and I'm very colour obsessiv which is probably a factor c having Asperger Syndrome. So, there isn't a separate 'playing with' gender: it's mixed in with being an artist being Aspie. Interestingly, since transitioning, I've add more earth colours to the previously predominant red and blues.

I came to my realisation that I was trans like a bolt of lightning, very suddenly. I had no prior warning. I had no long period of reflection, or contact with the trans community, to see if I fitted in. It just dropped out of the sky one day for me and I just jumped in with both feet, and ran ahead. I knew nothing, and I had no knowledge about anything; about medical aspects, social aspects, the history, the way that I could expect my friends and family to react, the discrimination that was out there. So, I immediately joined online communities, which at the time was the FTM UK Yahoo group. I'd check that every day, chat to people, read everything else that people were going through. I learned a lot of stuff about surgery and hormones and complications and waiting lists and how bad the clinics were and how messed up everything was in the health service. I very quickly cottoned onto the way people talk about it. I started seeing a free counsellor at the gender clinic in Scotland, where I was transitioning, and then started going to a support group there, which had been running for a really long time. It was a mixed support group and was just a lifeline really. I would just go along and stand very quietly and listen to everybody and not really say anything, and then go home. I couldn't have guessed that just being in a room with trans people would have such a huge impact on me, would be enough.

A lot of the time, I didn't need to talk, I didn't want to talk things through always. Just knowing that I had a place to go, while I figured things out and kind of got my head round what I was planning to do, was huge. I really relied on that and met some people and had face-to-face conversations. Getting the courage to say to somebody, "So, you've just started hormones. What does it feel like?" and "Are you scared?" and "Are you feeling good about it?".

Online stuff is great and it probably was huge for the trans community to be able to get online and start meeting up with each other around the UK, but face-to-face is different. It's really powerful and makes you feel normal. Scary too, but does make you feel normal. I think that visibility is one of the key ways to break down discrimination. The more projects that have trans people talking about themselves, talking about their lives, the more information there is out there for the next generation of trans people and their families and their friends and their business colleagues, the better. I didn't come out to people very often. The people who knew had known me already, and we didn't talk about it. Some people found out because people gossiped but I wouldn't really have classed myself as out. I didn't talk about it unless I absolutely had to and that was usually with doctors.

Ed

Nick

One of the reasons myself and a few buddies here in Brighton set up an FTM trans support group is because I've always been really, really aware that our issues are different from those of trans women. I think trans women experience possibly more verbal abuse and violence on the street, but what we suffer from really massively is invisibility. The reason that I transitioned quite late in life was because I actually didn't know it was possible. I didn't know that the medical technology existed to make it possible. And this is incredible to me because prior to that, I had a trans woman friend and we never talked about the fact that she was trans. She didn't want to talk about it and we were a circle of friends and we all knew, but we never talked about it with her.

There seems to be this ongoing debate between people who say "I'm trans, I'm always trans, I'm never going to be anything else" and people who say "Well, no, I have a trans history, I was trans, now I'm just a guy". For me, realistically I spent so much of my life before I transitioned, I don't think I will ever be able to say "I'm just a guy with a trans history". I'm very proud of my identity as a trans man. I suppose the thing about stealth is that it's about claiming the right not to have to proclaim your trans status from the rooftops all the time. I'm sensitive to that. I think it's also about something internal. There's a felt sense, in that if you're talking about sexuality and you're in the closet, really you actually know that you're lesbian, gay or bi but you're just not able, or don't want to, declare that. Whereas I think the difference with stealth is, if you have an internal sense of "I'm just a guy now", it almost feels artificial to be going around and making a big deal about being trans. There are subtle, but important differences.

Ultimately, I think you have to respect everybody's choices. I don't think stealth is possible for me, I'm too out there publicly. I'd have to go around the world to Australia or something. I think hiding important facts about yourself takes effort and I just can't be bothered to go stealth.

Dr Nick Douglas is an academic health researcher with an interest in trans health activism. A founder of FTM Brighton, he was the first Coordinator of the LGBT Health and Inclusion Project, which was influential in the founding of Trans Alliance.

Sam

I find it harder to be out as a Christian than as trans. Oddly enough, I find it really difficult to be out as a Christian in LGBT circles and I find it very difficult to be openly trans. Well, I don't really have much choice, it's kind of written on my forehead. But I do find it difficult in Christian circles to talk about my trans status.

I'm not one of those evangelical, crazy Christians. I just have a very strong faith which has always held me and kept me going and actually probably is the reason I'm still alive. So, it's important to me that we recognise that trans people can be Christian and there are no barriers, apart from our own barriers of shame and other people's treatment of us, which is pretty horrendous, a lot of the time.

I can trace my spiritual journey, if you like, as an adult. It mirrors my transition. So, in other words, the closer I am to god or the divine or the universe or whatever you want to call a higher power, the more I'm able to make this journey to authenticity. I've never felt, unlike a lot of people who are trans Christian, or gay and Christian, that who I am is fundamentally wrong.

I've never felt that it precludes me from participating in Christian church, or any other religious practice, but I know a lot of people do feel that, I know they feel as though these are two things that are completely incompatible. That has got an awful lot to do with the fact that Christianity, in particular, is deeply homophobic and, by definition, transphobic. I mean they wouldn't even make the separation, that's what's really fascinating. It's like walking into some antiquated environment where they've never even heard of some of the language that we use and trying to explain to people who I am, and what that means, when all they can think is god created man and woman and you can't have mixtures of the two, or anything in between.

It's really hardcore; you're trying to unpick someone's earliest value set if you like, and that's quite hard. So that process had to happen inside me first, obviously, which was pretty hard, that's probably when I was at my lowest in terms of coming out. I felt most suicidal when I was trying to shed that; you have to pare everything you believe down to the ground and start all over again, which was pretty hard work.

If you look at early church Christian teaching about the desert hermits, the early church fathers who wrote about the nature of god, they would say that knowledge of god or the divine is equal to knowledge, deep interior knowledge of the self. It makes sense to me then that the closer I feel to god or the divine, the closer I am to being true to myself.

I actually wrote to my sister the other day, trying to explain some things to her. I said to her that for the first time in my life, I was enjoying the feeling of being liked and being able to say to myself and say to her, I am a likeable person. I never, ever thought that before. I just felt I always had to prove that all the time, to do things for people. But the fact is that I now like myself and that's the difference. That's a lot to do with the sort of support and encouragement I had from people and friends, and not just trans friends by any means. It was that thing of just saying "Look, I know I'm not perfect, I'm not where I want to be in all sorts of way, but I'm not going to delay my life any longer. I am just going to, as best I can, be the best Alice I can be. That's all I can do". And that was just really such a relief.

The whole business of coming out was bloody painful. I went through weeks of agony. I was quite lucky with The Clare Project: it's always had a good counsellor there. It's enormously painful to be among friends and family thinking you're persona non grata, knowing that people are whispering about you behind your back. I think the world's different to me now, because it's brighter. To me it's more vibrant now, less threatening. I wake up every morning glad to be awake and I think a lot of transgender people spend quite big chunks of their lives waking up wishing they hadn't woken up, because that can happen. I'd say to people don't give in to it, because that's a very thin line that we tread. And I've not been shy about saying I got really near to falling off that edge a couple of times, and what happens if you don't is pretty wonderful.

Alice

Fox

Darcy

I think dress definitely has played a part. First of all, I think that it's nuts that you'd have to do this two year thing for someone else to tell you that you're trans. They might have actually abolished that now, because it's dangerous, too, if you can't take hormones then you put yourself into dangerous situations. For me, I was definitely exploring my gender, defining as a transvestite before embracing being transgender so drag kinging really did it for me. I just loved it so much. I remember seeing what people were up to in other towns and cities, like San Francisco or places in Australia as well. They just seemed so far ahead of where we were at in Brighton ten years ago.

The drag scene was a very exciting time. It actually did hit Brighton, probably around 2005/6. I don't see many drag kings any more and I think quite a few of the people who were drag kinging are actually transitioning now. So it was a safe space for packing and binding and putting on facial hair and doing all that felt really, really great. But It wasn't enough to make me feel like I could just take it all off and return to life as Rachel.

I came out as genderqueer when I was in my teens to pretty much everyone I knew, a term I no longer identify with. It's only been within the last few years that I've really started to feel comfortable in my male identity and came out to everyone as transsexual. It was quite a long process for me and I went through so many different stages over the years.

On reflection I think I was really scared to admit to myself that I was transsexual, I was happy to have a trans identity, but coming to terms with the fact that I'd need to make so many physical changes in order to be happy was overwhelming and hard for me to admit. I didn't feel like anyone had any expectations of how I should look or how I should act as someone who was genderqueer, but I was worried all that would change if I said I was a man.

I was really self-conscious for a long time after coming out before I started passing, it felt really uncomfortable for me knowing I was male, but no one else seeing me that way.

Passing has become more and more important to me. Since I've been on T, I haven't been misgendered by anyone in a very very long time, apart from a few fuck ups with old work colleagues, but I still don't feel confident in passing. I'm still convinced that I'll get misgendered, even when someone is referring to me as 'he' and 'sir' I'm sure they'll clock me eventually. Since I've accepted my identity and the processes I need to go through to reach a level of comfortability, everything just makes sense to me. The trans part of me is becoming more about my medical history, rather than a part of my identity.

Rebecca

When I came out at work it was like "Oh, that's a bit of a surprise." Previously, I came out as presenting as a gay male to cover up all my effeminacy, even though I've got a girlfriend. I used that as a kind of cover, or a bi-male as a cover, to be more socially acceptable. As a trans girl, I'd learnt to hide all my mannerisms because I got teased. The way I spoke was different and something didn't quite make sense to people about me. Saying that you're gay, you can get away with almost anything. The reaction to coming out as trans was generally very good. I think most people were trying their best, but it was like having cancer or a terminal illness or something where people don't really know what to say.

As a person, as myself, I didn't change at all. I was having laser treatment in the run up to it and I had started hormone treatment, but I still had to cover up some facial hair. I'd dropped a few hints to colleagues along the way, nobody got it of course, you have to be very direct. It was okay within the nursing team, but with doctors and people who move around in the hospital it was quite difficult. The patients were absolutely fine, none of them had that much of problem with me, but some of the other staff would stare at me which was quite uncomfortable.

I'm very lucky as a trans woman in my mid-thirties to transition and look fairly reasonable. I just count my blessings for that. To look in the mirror, I did it this morning, I got out of bed, I looked in the mirror and it's just relief. There's not much that changed on my body particularly. My hair's longer, and my skin's changed a little bit and my face has padded out a bit, but I'm just more comfortable. It is lovely to live your life as you want, from little things like opening my wardrobe, looking in and having beautiful things to wear; dresses, make up, perfume – and relating to people in a genuine way and being able to talk and express yourself naturally. All my life I'd looked at photographs and felt that something was wrong. I looked awkward. Now I look at my photographs and I'm seeing a woman there. It's fantastic.

Darcy Heston is a feminist trans man who loves sharks, cartoons and street art. He takes far too many selfies and hopes to grow a decent beard one day.

Chapter Five: Jumping Through Hoops.

Surgery, hormones, waiting, National Health Service, going private, legalities

Steph

I think one of the things you need to do is really sit down and work out what you want from it. I mean taking the transgender path. Don't take it until you're absolutely certain you have no doubts. Right at the very beginning it's possible to go back, but once you've started hormones it's quite difficult to go back, and once you've had the operation it's practically impossible to go back. For a lot of people there comes a time where living their life is so hard that the only option is to transition or harm yourself or commit suicide. But I would always, always prefer people to talk to groups like The Clare Project and get an awareness of exactly what steps they're taking.

Rory

When I started testosterone I was about twenty-seven and it was a really difficult two years settling into it, turning into a teenage boy. Being moody and spotty and having a croaky voice, I didn't especially enjoy being a teenager again and life was made better when I got an Xbox. Obviously, it's great to have the physical changes but it's really tough. I don't want to have to go through that again.

I never felt a really huge dysphoria like I imagined other people have but life was getting really hard being trans and not transitioning. So I decided to go and see the doctor to get a referral to Charing Cross Gender Identity Clinic which ended up being much quicker than I expected because they had cancellations. So in less than a year from seeing my GP, I was on T. I had had all those years of living as Rory so I did get prescribed testosterone on the second appointment because I had already done two or three years of real life experience. I am really glad I held off because it made that final journey much quicker.

Once I started taking T my relationship to my body changed and I was sick to death of binding so getting top surgery was brilliant. My relationship to other parts of my body has changed too but I still can't make a decision on what I want regarding further surgery. It's not just about my body, it's about my feelings towards undergoing more major surgery. Do I want to take this much time off work? I'm worried about recuperation times and stuff like that. Is this what I want

for my life? I feel like I've got to a point in my transition where I've achieved what I wanted out of it in terms of social presentation. My voice changing was the key thing, and getting stronger. I can go swimming in the sea. I can be topless publicly. I can go to the gym without worrying too much. The lack of other parts I can deal with. It does get me down sometimes.

I had everything through the NHS, I was super lucky. I think I managed to get in at the time it was still good, before it got completely screwed up by the Tories. I got through Charing Cross really quickly and got the thumbs up for top surgery a year later. I ended up seeing the surgeon of my choice who happened to be local, and I had it at the Nuffield Hospital rather than having to go to a NHS hospital. It was Andrew Yelland who's just a lovely bloke. He did a surgical procedure he'd never done on a trans person before and basically just sucked it out. I don't have scars which is amazing and I've still got the original parts that sort of work.

I think most people have things they don't like about the results of their surgery. Unfortunately because of the type of surgery I had I don't have a flat chest. I've got a chest that any bloke my size and shape is going to have. It was keyhole surgery; a tiny little incision about two to three inches below the nipple and two to three inches at the side of the nipple where the keyhole things go in. They just sucked out the fats which has flattened my chest. I don't have any regrets about that.

Sarah

One of the things that held me back from transitioning was the thought that I had to have lower surgery. Then I learnt that not all trans people live to this binary and some trans people only go so far in medical transition. I'd been reading on the internet for years about how the NHS will dictate this route and if you deviate from it a little bit, then you're not trans. That's been a complete eye-opener to me. Now I don't even bother to try and change my voice. I'm a lot more comfortable in my skin, because of the hormones that I've got. The insecurities that I've got about my body are outweighed by the feeling of happiness that the hormones give me.

It took me eighteen months of living full time as female before I got onto hormones, because I was moving about so much and I didn't get to Charing Cross. But I've been twice now and seen doctors who are supposedly terrible and both times they've been really nice. I've been able to approach them with any concerns or worries that I've had. They said to me "What do you want out of this?"

And I said, "Well, I want some hormones, please". And they said, "Come back in three months, you seem to have fulfilled the criteria so far and you can probably have some."

I've been completely blown away by how different my perception was and the reality actually is. I had the anti-androgen injection which lasts for three months and apart from decreased sex drive I didn't feel all that much to start with. I stopped taking it for three months because I couldn't really tell a difference, maybe it happened so gradually. I felt the testosterone kicking back in, and then all the feelings that I used to have came flooding back. So I had an extra injection. Then I came off them again, for a month, just before Christmas, just to make doubly sure that I knew what I was doing and it was the right thing for me. Within a month this time I knew. They've made me feel calm, bringing a sense of serenity. It's the subtlest of differences, but it has such a huge effect. If I won the Lottery I'd get some facial surgery and I'd get my hair fixed.

I did an internet search. There is a risk that what you're getting is not what it says it is, so you're wasting your money, or it might do you some harm. I did research on prescriptions and what levels the hormones needed to be. I settled on a particular supplier and used my knowledge about public health to work out whether what I was being supplied with were genuine pharmacy products. I felt happy, I felt peaceful. My anxieties disappeared, and in the last nine years, I haven't suffered from anxiety at all. I just felt normal, the way it should have been all my life.

People stared, and some people spoke, in the early years. You realise it's not your fault they're doing that. It's their fault, they don't know any better. I grew my hair. I did have laser hair removal treatment on my face, quite early on, but I couldn't afford to keep that going. Physically my body shape changed as a result of the hormones. My emotional responses changed, I became very creative, more empathetic, more understanding and tolerant. I lost a lot of muscle mass, and I dropped a size and a half in shoes. My breasts started to grow, my sexual function disappeared, but it was fine, because I was getting what I wanted out of it. After a few years I thought, "You can't just keep

buying stuff off the internet, apart from the cost of it, at some point you have to be monitoring and maintaining your health". So I went to see my doctor and got referred for a clinical assessment.

Now I'm a patient at the Charing Cross Gender Identity Clinic. It's frustrating, to say the least. My difficulty is I transitioned on my own without any assistance other than the support of a few friends. I've been living as the woman I am today for almost ten years, and I've managed to do seven years of that without the GIC. Their system's set up to cope with people who are right at the beginning of their transition and they can't get their heads round it. They wanted to treat me as if I was a new patient, and follow the stages and steps that a new or recently transitioned person would. It's way too far gone for me. I've been living as a woman since 2005, yet they want me to prove it.

I sold my house last year and I moved into rented and I'm using the equity from the property to pay for the remainder of my transition, which is mainly the physical aspect. In June last year, I had a breast enlargement operation. In July this year, I'm having my gender reassignment surgery. I'm paying for it privately and all the

assessments that lead up to it, because I waited ten months for my first appointment at the Gender Identity Clinic. Then another six months for my second one, to be told, unless you can prove that you've been living as a woman for more than twelve months, that your next appointment will not be a referral for surgery, it will just be another clinical assessment. Thanks very much, NHS.

There are a lot of trans people in Sussex. In particular in the Brighton area, yet there are no services directly accessible here. You have to go to London. My GP is very understanding and supportive. There's a shared care agreement between her and my private gender specialist, and they're managing my hormones and monitoring my health which makes me feel happier. Being on hormones long term, there are health risks, but it's a necessity. I'm using the equity from the sale of the property to fund private treatment, before I hit fifty. I have to deal with it. I have to complete the physical transformation. If I want to have any chance of a life with a loving partner, and to have a happy rest of my life then I came to the conclusion I needed to do it. Just transitioning roles wasn't enough.

Gloria

Joanna

Luc

I went to my GP who was a Christian and not sympathetic at all. She said, "I can't do anything". She was a member of the same church I was attending and she told the church pastor. That was it, I was excluded from the church. It was a very evangelical church, and they didn't approve of anything LGBT at all. Maybe they've changed their tune now, but I suspect not. This church was quite strong on their particular beliefs about sexuality and they treated transgender as being a sexuality thing, which of course is rubbish.

I then went to the Gender Trust and said, "Where do I find a trans-friendly doctor?" And they told me to go to the Ship Street surgery. This was brilliant and I got completely supported. They referred me first to the local mental health team. I saw a psychiatrist, he turned round to me and said, "Okay, fine. I can see that you're serious about changing gender. Please tell me what to do, who to refer you to." So I said, "Well, you're supposed to refer me to Charing Cross Gender Clinic." He did that, and so the process slowly started.

It wasn't until I was forty-eight that I started my transition via the southwest GIC and had an initial radical mammoplasty surgery to 'gender-neutralise' my body. Later I started taking testosterone as topical gel, when I realised that I needed to have masculine physiology on the outside to express what I experienced on the inside: my transintersexuality. I've been going to Charing Cross GIC, over some eighteen months recently, because I had a request to be approved for further surgery to masculinise my chest so that it matched the fact that I was taking T and getting some chest hair – to go with the now-hairy legs that I used to have recurring dreams about.

I have identified more with the trans-masculine side now, probably because the T changes your psyche: it does bring in more 'male' thinking. I think too that it's a reflection of my age: I'd done fifty years trying to be okay as female, and I've had enough. I will be having, effectively, a double mastectomy in July this year.

I just followed the given NHS pathway back then; fifteen years ago now. I hadn't really thought about the lower surgery. I just knew that I wanted to get rid of my chest. A lot of guys missed having a penis. I never really felt like that. I just thought, "Get rid of these disgusting things and if you don't, I'll cut them off myself". It wasn't a very common operation back then; I had to wait six years between starting the hormones and having the actual chest surgery. That was quite a hellish time, because I was getting the facial hair, the voice was dropping, I was getting the body hair, I'd changed my name and people were reading me as a guy, but I was still having to strap the chest down. It was just very, very uncomfortable and restricted me, both physically and mentally, in everything I did.

One of the nurses told me when you first start on hormones you become ten times more horny than most cisgendered guys. I don't know whether that's true or not, but that's the way I felt. I did get very angry and had a lot of pent up aggression when I first went onto the testosterone. It was fantastic once I got into my long-term relationship though, being so horny, it was amazing. I didn't realise quite how big the mood swings would be though. I wish someone had told me that. A year or so after that, I started looking into having the radial artery forearm flap phalloplasty surgery. I had the first operation, here in the UK, in 2008. I've had a lot of problems, both with the surgery and infections. I didn't feel things were explained or done properly.

I now always say to anyone who's planning on having the phalloplasty surgery; do as much research as you can. The best thing to do is talk to people who've actually had it done already. I've had fourteen operations now, over the last five years, and as I said, it's still not finished. It takes an overwhelmingly massive toll on you, and on all those closest to you; not only your physical health, but equally on your mental health too. It's caused a lot of extremely bad depression and resentment. I feel like my life's being held back.

Ben

Initially went to my GP in Brighton, I told them I was transsexual and that I needed to start medically transitioning. They were realistic about how long it would be until I could access hormones and have surgery. By this point my dysphoria had gotten so bad that I'd been off work for a few months with social anxiety and depression, it was affecting all aspects of my life, not just work, but friends, family, my relationship, everything. I was at a point that I needed medical intervention, I needed to access treatment. Waiting even a month at that point would have felt like an eternity, so to be told it could be well over a year until anything happens was just devastating. I couldn't afford to, but I went private at this point.

The process was so quick and straight-forward, I called up Dr Curtis at the Transhealth Clinic in London and got my first appointment within two weeks. He sent me away with a report for my GP, instructions for them to do some blood tests and advised me to have an appointment with a gender therapist in the mean time. I got the go ahead for T at my next appointment about a month later. Privately transitioning can be very expensive, I was lucky that my GP was happy to do all of the necessary blood work and prescribe my T on Dr Curtis's recommendation, it was just the appointments which were the big expense at the time. But I feel very lucky and realise how privileged I am compared to many who just don't have that option.

I'd decided years ago that if I could, I'd have my top surgery with Dr Garramone in Florida. I'm in debt now as a result but it was the best decision I ever made. It's changed my life drastically. I had such a huge sense of relief and my mind was suddenly free to think about things other than surgery which I'd been focused on for so long. Realising how much damage dysphoria had done over the years and examining other parts of my life that had been put on hold as a result gave me major post op blues, wishing I'd have transitioned years ago. Bottom surgery is now on my mind more than ever, I know it's something I need but right now I'm enjoying life free of appointments and surgery anxieties and in all honesty I'm just really scared of putting myself through that right at this point.

Darcy

Rebecca

They sent me completely the wrong drug. What's that drug called? It's to maintain erections. Viagra, that's it. So I'm sitting there with these tablets of Viagra and I'm shaking. I've still got them, these Viagra things, why would I want to do that to myself?

I eventually started on HRT and T-blockers then upped my oestrogen after three months. It was all self-prescribed and illegal but I could function. The immediate psychological relief was stopping my testosterone. I know that I'm not going to suddenly turn into some little princess, but as you get older you get even more masculine, and I'd reached that point in my mid-thirties where that process was starting. It was intolerable for me.

I know this probably sounds a bit weird but I took my little oestrogen tablet, and I was laying in the bath and I felt my muscles just twitch a little bit all over. It was almost like popping under my skin. Then you have that whole euphoria. I was dressing part time as a woman. I wasn't out at work. This is about three months into my transition. I'd started laser hair removal and working on my voice. I felt more confident as a woman as soon as I had that little bit of oestrogen on board. I could relate to my gender and the world from a much better place, be more emotionally aware. It was a fantastic feeling, a real high. On a physical level not having to deal with male physiology and

male physiological drives was an enormous benefit. As a trans woman, those demands on you are incredibly confusing, damaging and hurtful to grow up with. I can't quite describe how awful it makes you feel. Having that stop and not being driven by it is an incredible relief.

I asked the psychiatrist if he could give me a rough time-scale so that I can cope with waiting for help. I've heard that there's a nine month waiting list and I'm due to see my third psychiatrist in February, so it maybe that I'm waiting until I'm forty to have corrective surgery. That's really tough because I'm living my life as a woman. What you wear is restricted because you've got a lump in the middle, and having a wee is awful, because you've got to put up with it. I have an intimate sexual relationship with my partner, and I want her to relate to me as a woman. I know I'm not going to get a proper, one-hundred percent functioning, perfect-looking vagina. What I'm getting is a vaginoplasty. It's not self-lubricating, you have to look after it, it takes a lot of care. But it will look better and I'll be happier with it. The other thing is that I just need to get rid of those testosterone producing things that made me wrong in the first place. My big fear is that I'm going to go backwards. I'll suddenly turn into a guy and wake up and it'll all be a dream and that terrifies me. God, I talk too much about vaginas at the moment.

In the current protocol for health care it would have taken two plus years to get prescribed HRT. I was at a stage where I was literally screaming inside and I couldn't wait any longer. I did my research on the internet, being a nurse helps and gives you a bit more confidence. I started myself on a low dose of oestrogen from the internet and a testosterone blocker. I was absolutely desperate. I found a pharmacy in India online, and I did my order. I paid for extra fast delivery because I was beside myself.

Ed

I'd deliberately not done loads of research into all the different hormones and surgeries that were out there, because I wanted to come to my own conclusions, without taking up other people's ideas. Being trans is having a gender identity that doesn't match with my body and therefore having to snip and chop and inject things in order to have a body that is bearable. It still doesn't feel like it's my body though. It's just a body that is more bearable than the one that I was born with. So I'm incredibly grateful that transitioning exists, and is on the NHS. God knows where I'd be if I had to pay for any of this myself and not been able to. I'm really glad to have transitioned, but I wouldn't have chosen it over having a gender identity that matched my body. I got really excited about looking more male, feeling more myself, coming into my own skin. That was a really lovely experience, but I would have rather have just had it in the first place, or just been happy being a woman.

I've only been in Brighton four years. I'm now using Charing Cross, but for the bulk of the first stages I used Sandyford. It was oddly smooth, as a process. It works very differently from London. I figured out I was trans one night, I told my psychiatrist the next week. A week later I went to see my GP and said, "Hello, has my psychiatrist been in touch with you?" and she said, "Yes. I hear you want to change gender. You'll be needing to go to Sandyford then. Hang on a sec, I'll make you an appointment," and

picked up the phone. The way that Sandyford worked was that they had a drop-in session, monthly – although you could make an appointment and actually see one of the specialists if you wanted to.

It was totally different from all the other clinics that I've known about. I had an initial appointment with one of the psychologists for the big assessment. He asked me loads of questions and then gave me the diagnosis. But about six months into my real life experience, the head of the clinic became concerned that I'd had an eating disorder as a teenager. She said, "This is just a manifestation of that eating disorder. So we're going to start you over. Start again from the beginning". I sat in that room with her for three hours. I went home and got drunk and then wrote a letter the next day that said; "This is my trans history." I looked back over my teenage life and my childhood and it was blatantly obvious. I had loads of big flashing signals that I was trans and was going to transition.

After that I started hormones within the first year. I got three months taken off my real life test, for good behaviour. And then had top surgery within a year of that. Then I just sort of dropped off the trans spectrum. I didn't go to the support groups, I didn't see my trans friends. I didn't get involved in any LGBT things. I wasn't stealth. Loads of my friends knew, but we just didn't talk about it.

I went to see my GP in March. I was this absolute ball of anxiety and fear and pain that I've been carrying round with me. As soon as I went to see my GP, I felt like I'd just put this burden down. It was the sense of me doing something proactive for myself, reaching out and saying "I'm trans, can I have some help, please". Allowing myself to look after myself rather than just trying to be this stubborn hard arse. "No, it doesn't matter. It doesn't apply to me. I'm fine, I'm fine, I'm fine", which I'd been doing for years.

I said to my GP "I've got this cough" and she said, "Okay, well, I'll give you some medicine". Then I said, "Oh, and after twenty years of careful consideration, can I have a reference to the gender clinic, please?" And she just went "Hmm, yeah." Then she just started typing and I said, "Are you sure you're not going to...? I feel like there should be a bit of levity to this situation". And she just took her glasses off and turned and looked at me, and just went "Darling, I've been a GP in this town for twenty years". And I was like "Okay". She didn't bat an eyelid.

Maeve

E-J

I've had to get hormones any way I can wherever I am no matter what. I had 6 month hormone implants in Melbourne but my body rejected them and they came out when I was in Vietnam so I bought T there over the counter.

At the airport in Sydney they thought I was using my T vials to smuggle drugs, kept me for hours, threatened to strip search me and made me miss my connecting flight to my granddad's funeral.

In Tokyo, I hooked up with the trans group that was being run a million floors up in a skyscraper... I got out of the lift and there were ten trans Japanese guys! I used to see an illegal doctor in Shinjuku who'd make me strip and wear a medical gown and lie down for my injections. Surreal.

When I lived in Madrid there was a big scene there for girls to go into sex work to finance surgery and once they'd had it they'd go off the game. It was like a scene from an Almodovar film - beautiful, powerful and dark all at the same time. In Singapore there's trans girls living in these little empty cement boxes down long, eerie, redlight district alleys and they sit in the shadows together laughing and smoking fags.

Trans surgery is becoming a class issue as more and more people go private or to the black market because access to treatment is so slow and often fundamentally demeaning in the process. Here in Brighton, if waiting lists don't get shorter we'll eventually have our class status physically written in trans scars across our hearts... 'Pretty private surgery got fast' versus the mental and physical effects of waiting for long periods to get surgery in a system that's increasingly under pressure to provide rushed procedures with less skilled practitioners. We need to start worrying about who is accessing what healthcare, where.

Public health systems around the world saved my little trans toosh. The NHS didn't just give me surgery, it gave me back my sense of self and a vision of the future. Not everyone's journeys are about surgery, but it's been a crucial part of mine. I've got my tits at home pickled in formaldehyde in glass jars as proof. They look fittingly grotesque and are precisely where they belong.

Nick

I'm a health researcher by training. I became a trans activist specifically because I had such massive concerns about the situation of trans people in relation to equal access to healthcare. Not only the trans care pathway but also basic access to primary care. We're unfortunately still not at a place where trans people can take it as read that they'll be treated equally or even respectfully and that's something that really drives me.

I am a massive supporter of the NHS and my experience had always been good until I started the pathway for gender reassignment. This is not like anything else in the NHS. Generally, you have a consent-based model. You're diagnosed with a problem and provided that you're competent and able to consent, and the treatment is deemed to be effective and necessary, you will get that treatment. It's completely different in the trans care pathway. What's there instead is this process of jumping through hoops set by psychiatrists, or what they disingenuously call 'standards of care'. It's an entirely different approach to medicine and it has really weird and often damaging

consequences. For instance, I was completely coerced into changing my name before I was ready, in order to get the hormones that I needed.

I've become more clued up and more assertive since then and I've also been quite fortunate in being able to find clinicians that I can work with and who will work with me. But certainly at the outset of the process, it was an absolute nightmare.

In any other field of medicine, some of the things I have experienced and heard of would be regarded as malpractice but because people are terrified of being 'punished' by having their treatment made impossible and access to what they need denied they put up with it. Or they're so grateful for any treatment at all and have such internalised transphobia they don't think they are entitled to anything better.

The only person who can really ascertain whether or not you are trans is you, which is why the whole diagnosis issue is absurd. That's why I'm very much a proponent of a consent-based model, which they're experimenting with in parts of the US. As a grown adult, as long as I am capable to consent to those procedures, then that should be all that's required.

Historically, trans medicine has been managed within a mental health framework, particularly psychiatry, which does not have a proud history in terms of dealing with queer people per se. Look at aversion therapy and shock therapy and those kinds of things. Psychiatry is

absolutely the wrong place for this kind of medicine to be located. Unfortunately, a lot of psychiatrists in this area are still in the very traditional mode of the powerful doctor making decisions for the sick patient. But the thing is I'm not sick and I certainly don't need anyone else making those decisions for me.

I've really struggled with the imposition of a mental health diagnosis because I needed to transition. That was and remains challenging for me, I'm still angry about the fact that it's such a waste of resources. There are people with mental health problems who really could use the help of good, sympathetic psychiatrists and those people should have access to that resource. Instead, it's being misused to sporadically, inadequately and repeatedly 'assess' people in the gender identity clinics when other clinicians and professionals could actually be helping, supporting and enabling us. Nurses, counsellors, social workers, couples therapists could be doing a massively better, more efficient and compassionate job, but the money is being wasted on expensive psychiatrists that the vast majority of us don't need.

What I needed was access to the means to transition: hormones, surgery, full-stop. What I got was endless spurious 'assessment', gate-keeping, delay and obstruction and no mental health support whatsoever. I would say I've seen some good individual clinicians (especially endocrinologists and surgeons), but the treatment model for getting access to them was bizarre and harmful.

Sam

I had a choice, as a doctor. I could afford to go privately, and I did see a private physician at the beginning but I decided that I would go with the NHS. Partly because breaks in the journey have been good for me, those moments where you can't do anything because you're just on a waiting list. These are moments when you plateau psychologically and you may need to breakthrough a barrier, let go of shame or crap from the past or some family stuff you need to deal with. So the slowness of that journey, I really appreciate it. Sadly I'm going to plump on the side of my medical colleagues and say that it's really okay to wait.

I meet so many trans people who are desperate to make physical changes but ninety-five percent of transition is all the mental and emotional stuff. Like letting go of the fact that you've been raised amongst women, but you don't really understand them. Then realising that you haven't got all that nurture to equip you for a life amongst men. So actually you're always going to end up somewhere in between. I've been lucky enough to have good therapy and work my way through a lot of it. If I hadn't done that, I think I'd be in a much worse state. I think sometimes that's why people are in a bad way when they're transitioning because they haven't had the time or the capacity or the resources to do the psychological work. It would be nice if the waiting lists were a bit shorter and if there was more access, but you see that across the NHS. It's true of any kind of medical provision in this country. I think the thing that's sadly lacking is the psychotherapeutic help. It's very difficult for people to live in role without any medical treatment, but I think it's probably crucial to do it.

I will challenge the system if I find that I'm being treated differently to other people. That would really make me mad. What I do know is that the gender clinics are doing an amazing job, and the guys that work there are stuck between a rock and a hard place. They're almost as much maligned by the rest of the medical fraternity who think we're all mad and shouldn't have our treatment on the NHS. So they suffer transphobia as well. They're worthy of our respect for the battles they're fighting. As far as we're concerned they're not doing enough. But as far as the rest of NHS believes, they're doing way too much to help a bunch of mad people. More power to the gender clinics. I'd like to get our own one in Brighton. If I could achieve that before I die I'll have done a good thing.

Dr Sam Hall is a transman, single parent and doctor living and working in Brighton. He has three children and a part-time job as a consultant anaesthetist. He is chair of the Clare Project and co-chairs the City Council's trans needs assessment panel.

Cass Hoskins was born in Brighton in 1968 and has lived here since the early 90's. A graphic designer who has worked in digital media for 20 years, she's a single parent who started her transition four years ago.

Chapter Six: I accept it's a mistake, but don't make it that often, please.

Safety, abuse, fear, violence, mis-gendering, barriers

Gloria

The supermarket queue for the till is the kind of classic, or the queuing up to pay for something in a shop. After three or four years I kind of looked very feminine, so just to look at me and walk past me in the street you wouldn't have known, but in those days my voice was still very deep. So when I spoke it gave it away a bit. You'd get people nudging each other, or you'd get people saying "That's a man", you know. It felt hurtful, yeah, it felt nasty. I mean most of the time it wasn't done in a nasty way. It was done in a very innocent, lack of knowledge way more than anything. I have been lucky I have not really suffered from transphobia to any great extent. I mean, I know other trans people who are not that lucky. Other people's lives have been blighted by hate and just a kind of real venom towards them, but I have been lucky in that respect.

I have suffered it a bit from time to time. For a long time I did work with gypsies and travellers – and they're the first to play the race card, the minority card – but in my experience there's racism and transphobia and homophobia in all races and all minorities. It's probably about the same percentage in all of them. I had problems with some of the traveller men. They were very anti, but I had a job to do, you know. I'm a northerner, I am thick skinned and I'm five-foot-nine as well, so, you overcome it don't you? You just think "Well, okay, if I'd been born a woman I would still get that sort of thing. I'd still get misogynistic comments. I'd still get people behaving that way towards me." So I kind of thought, "it isn't really any different. Just the words they're saying are different, but the meaning behind it is not any different."

Eli

I work in a school and the gender binary feels so ingrained in the schools, especially if you're a member of staff. You get called "Miss" or "Sir" the whole time, and if they say "Sir" they apologise straight afterwards. It's like "Really? Okay, fine", but it also means that if I transition, then it's like who I do I tell first? There's going to have to be the bit where I tell them "it's Sir now, not Miss", or do I just carry on not correcting them whichever one they say? If there wasn't binary in place I probably just wouldn't worry about it that much. Whereas actually it's like every day, like each lesson they probably say "Miss, Miss" about, I don't know, one-hundred times. So, you get it all day every day. And that probably makes the desire to actually do something about it stronger.

Eli is a teacher who lives in Brighton and works in East Sussex. They're a sci-fi fan who recently acquired a Star Trek uniform and they're currently watching 'Fringe'.

Cass

You can choose to be embarrassed by stuff and you can choose to be scared of stuff, or you can choose to let the fear stop you. It's like, I hate heights, but I will go up the Eiffel Tower if I'm in Paris. Actually when you get to the top it's fine, it's really nice and you go "Wow. Isn't Paris beautiful?" I wasn't going to let the fear stop me. The more you do it the more you realise there's not that much to fear.

Once, in London on the bus – and that was like my second time I ever went out in daylight, I think, as a woman – this guy was walking down the bus and he was hitting on everyone on the bus. He looked drunk and he was a bit scary and so I just kind of turned away, looking out the window. It was one of these bendy-buses, and you could see him coming all the way down the bus. When he got to me, 'cos I turned away and

was looking out the window, he stepped right in front of my face. He wanted to get my attention. And as soon as he got in front of my face he started shouting and screaming and calling me a freak and a pervert. He stood back in the middle of the bus, declaiming at me. As if like now he'd pointed it out to the rest of the bus that I was trans, the rest of the bus would kind of rise up and lynch me or something. But the rest of the bus just kind of scowled at him and ignored him, as typical Londoners. And I just carried on ignoring him and he got off the bus.

When you tell people who aren't trans, about those things, they're often quite shocked. I was talking to a colleague about a bar that everyone was going to and I said, "I don't feel comfortable in that bar because the people in there are a bit Neanderthal." And she said, "Well, fuck them then." I said, "It doesn't work like that, because it's me who's unhappy, it's not them. I don't make them unhappy. So it's just a miserable night for me, it's not a miserable night for them. So there's no point in me going 'Fuck you,' and having that attitude. Actually if you're in an environment that feels hostile, it doesn't work."

When I was at the beginning the stress, the social anxiety of just going into a pub, it was exhausting. I remember being exhausted almost

all the time just because of that day-to-day interaction with the world. What people would think and whether people saw through you and whether that mattered, the calculations that were going through my head. Talking about that, or having people around me that understand that is a thing I miss.

One of the things that really struck me about the reaction to trans women, particularly, is that I know lots of men who have lesbian friends, because it's all right: they're one of the lads. You hear people talk about someone who's gay and say "You wouldn't know they were gay." So, it's okay, they're not camp, they're not effeminate, they're not feminine, they're just like anyone else. I remember feeling like being trans is like this really extreme version of being feminine or making such a big deal about being feminine.

The reaction to someone being trans is more about rejection of manhood, it is almost like you've rejected masculinity, that you've abandoned it. It's a kind of misogyny, which is really interesting because it's just not about sexuality, it is about femininity. I think that was a real surprise for some in the gay community. They have as much a problem with very feminine gay men as they do with the trans community, because it's like 'don't scare the straights'.

Joanna

I went and spoke to a Jewish friend, Miriam, she's very supportive. She had heard that I had been cross dressing, coming out, but it was almost furtive. I wasn't coming out in the day, and she said, "Jo, you're coming with me to Tesco" and she took me shopping at Tesco, in broad daylight. I was with her and her children. Nobody really made anything of it but I was terrified. So I started going out as Jo, going over to my friends, playing Bridge with them, all local. We lived on a council estate.

Then one day a gang of people went round to my friend's house and beat on the door, while we were playing Bridge. They were saying, "Bring out the paedophile." They were a mob, and they had baseball bats and whatever. My friend said, "What?" and they explained that I was actually transgendered and that had nothing to do with paedophilia, not anything like that. And the penny dropped and most of them were going "Oh, we made a mistake." They'd been incited to do this by one particular family on the estate who were intolerant of homosexuals, intolerant of Jews and intolerant of black people, so I was just the next target. This wasn't in Brighton, this was in Lancing, and I fled from Lancing to here.

I had discussed with my colleagues I was coming to work from January 2000 as Jo. The turn of the millennium, a new me. It was good, and I started seeing my colleagues as Jo, in social situations. We were out on a ten-pin bowling night and I think they were expecting me to walk in with a miniskirt, high heels and traditional 'tranny' image. But no, I was wearing jeans and sneakers. They were going "We thought you'd be dolled up" and I said, "To play ten pin bowling?". The girls were just laughing at that, so, I thought, "Success", and as I went out, one of my colleagues' sons – not my colleague himself but his adult son – turned round to me and said, "You're a fucking pervert. You're fucking sick." He said that straight into my face and then just walked off. I was just shocked and it sort of took me from a high, straight down to a low, almost immediately. You just have to put it to one side, you can't let it drag you down.

Things just steadily proceeded at work, I was eventually accepted, but they told me I had to use the disabled toilet in the basement because one colleague in the entire company complained about me using the ladies. They said, "When you've had the operation, then you can use the women's toilet." I didn't realise how discriminatory it was, but I thought, "Do I rock the boat? No. I'm accepted, I don't want to make big waves".

Ruth

On Monday I went to the police committee that they've set up to guide them through the way that they deal with people in custody. I'm sitting there with half a dozen others, giving them advice and making sure that they're doing the right thing: they're asking us because they really are open to doing it right. That sort of thing is, from my point of view, double-edged, because I'm doing it from the transgender community's point of view and from those who are older people who are caught up in the transgender thing as well. I mean if an older person is arrested by the police, and they happen to be transgendered, then I'm the only person there that can speak as one of them.

I have sat in on cases where transgendered people have been in court, for one reason or another, just as an observer, to make sure that what is being done is within the law and within what we would call proper justice. It has changed now, but about six years ago I went to an appalling case. Somebody who had been living for something like eight or ten years as a woman was in court with a charge of assault against her. She had been spat at by some people who knew she was transgendered, in a public place and beaten

up by them. She had retaliated and pushed one to the ground and then was accused by this person of assaulting them. The police took out an assault charge against her and in court referred to her as "him" with the male pronoun. The police did and the prosecution did. It was disgusting.

A lot of doctors' surgeries, as you go in, have an appointments touch screen. You can put your details in if you have an appointment. The screen asks "Are you male or are you female?" so what do I say? My doctor is in charge of the fact that I changed from male to female, but when I put female in, it says it can't find me and when I put male in, it says it can't find me. If you have an appointment at the doctors, does it matter whether you're male or female? All you're booking in is the fact that you have arrived for your appointment. It's those sort of things, they're subtle things, but they are irritatingly abusive by their passivity against us. They have an assumption that we're still outsiders from normal society and we want to break that assumption down. We want recognition that we can be anything we need to be in society, and our gender is not that important.

m lucky I'm a trans bloke, I'll say that straight out. I am so lucky that I pass, I'm such a small guy. My life is hard enough as it is, I've been beaten up four times in Brighton, and it's been gay bashings, because I pass as a man and they say things like "So you're one of them Brighton faggots is ya?". It's hard enough being small, but I can't imagine what it would be like if I didn't pass, how that would change how easily I could integrate and function within society. I would be so intimidated and so scared all the time, I think, I would have a lot more problems than I do now.

The one grace that I have is that I pass, so people don't stare and point. It would crush me and I would get myself into all kinds of trouble, because I can't help but stand up for myself and fight back against discrimination and point blank rudeness. There are so many brave people who choose to live in the middle of the gender spectrum, because it's right for them. It takes extraordinary courage. I just have so much respect for them, but, you know, you can't do anything about it. You've just got to get on with life, don't you?

I had a job, quite a high-flying job in Tokyo as a creative production manager. But at that stage I was female on my passport and I had to show them my passport to get paid. So there was a period of being closeted mid-transition. I ended up finishing that job and then falling off the employment bandwagon because I couldn't see how I could be employed while my passport was female. I looked

male and my voice was breaking and I was starting to grow facial hair, so, that was really tough. I was completely isolated from integrating with society on a professional level and I was very used to being a professional. That took ten years out of my professional development. I also had a high-flying career in Australia before I decided to transition; I was an award-winning writer, I was senior creative writer for one of the two national radio networks, I was doing so much stuff at such a young age and really achieving high end. Then I just had to walk away and let it all go.

There was no way for me to catch up on my professional career again, so financially I've just gone backwards. I find it very hard to live with. It's something that I'm so conscious of, that I don't own a house, that I don't have a pension or savings, it keeps me awake at night. It scares the living daylights out of me and makes me deeply disappointed in myself because that's not who I thought I was going to be. So I feel embarrassed and scared and insecure.

For people to not have to go through that journey that ruins their career, we need to, on the one hand, provide trans awareness education, both within the workplace and within the education system for teachers, and on the other, let kids transition as soon as they can so they can get on with their lives and careers

uninterrupted. Let's face it, so many trans people are so very talented, clever and have the potential to become high achievers. We oughtn't be a burden on society, we should be given the chance to be, and increasingly are, social leaders. It's in our genes, I tell you, it seems to be a reoccurring part of our innate mix. Perhaps it's a result of having to be so brave, so deeply self-analytical and so socially aware.

E-J

I think one of the reasons I didn't transition earlier is because I'm a doctor. I know how a white, male, middle class, heterosexual, privileged doctor thinks. That's my context and my background so I understand how and why they think the way they do. I basically got to the point where I was ready to leap under a train and it was suicidal idealisation that drove me to get on and do the formal transition at work. I was terrified of how people would react and I was right to be terrified of it, because there was a bad reaction and people did persecute me. I've spent the best part of the last eighteen months fighting that and it's been really hard. I think the medical model of gender dysphoria is still a mental health one, sadly. Doctors, unless they know better, have a kind of almost a knee-jerk reaction: that we're a little bit mad.

Prejudice is really covert these days, you don't see it, it's like an invisible snaky type thing that you can't quite get a handle on, but people start to exclude you or treat you differently and it took me a while to figure that it was actually happening. I find that really regrettable, but I also think that it spurred me to do something to make changes. I do know other doctors that have transitioned and most of them tend to keep their heads below the parapet, but in the small amount of trans activism that I am involved in that's one of my biggest soapboxes, educating my colleagues. I'm in the midst of an employment tribunal in the workplace. The reason I'm doing it is because I want it written in black and white that I've been discriminated against on account of my trans status. I just want to see that for my own self-worth and self-respect. If, in the process I manage to make a bit of case law and change history in one tiny way, that's great, but I can't afford for that to be my motive.

Sam

When I was perceived to be a non-gender-conforming person I felt very differently about my safety. I never actually had a bad experience, but was just very conscious of the fact that people noticed me. As passing became a reality that all changed, I personally feel very safe in Brighton as someone who's now read as male. The fact that I'm white, able bodied and perceived to be heterosexual also plays a part in that. The main issue was that for a long time I was being mis-gendered by 'friends', many of whom I no longer see as a result.

My workplace overall was very supportive, but the issue of pronouns has been an ongoing battle that only recently has been resolved. I changed all my details a few years ago and didn't expect this to still be happening. I felt like I did let people off lightly for so long, as I felt super awkward correcting people when I was so conscious of the fact that I didn't pass as male. That shouldn't matter of course, that was my own internal bullshit. We have lots of new people working for us now who didn't know me before, so I've been outed on a number of occasions by those that have been with the company longer. I had a meeting with them about this recently and they are taking it seriously, so we'll see what happens. I'm definitely more confident now to pull people up on it, but to be honest I'm getting to the point that I'm uncomfortable with anyone in my work place even knowing about my history, even those that don't fuck up. I'm not treated any differently but I'd much rather be in a workplace where that's not something anyone is aware of.

Darcy

Rebecca

For that six months transitionary phase, it was very difficult with people staring at me and, as far as I gather, my boss had explained to everybody that I was trans and that I should be referred to in these gender pronouns and what have you, but they got it wrong. Every single day that I walked into work for six months I was called by my old name, or my old gender pronoun, and that had a very deleterious effect on my mental health, unfortunately. It tailed off naturally because when you take HRT and your body and your face feminises – and I have no facial hair – it starts to become ridiculous to call someone who looks like a woman a man. It tails off by itself. People obviously tried very hard, but, when you're presenting as female to patients and families, and then someone calls you 'Bob', or something, it's excruciatingly painful because it puts you back to that position where you couldn't come out. It was a very, very painful thing to hold in for so long.

Rory

I identify as genderqueer. I don't mind people seeing me as male because to be fair I look, sound and present as male, that's absolutely fine. I'd rather they do that than see me as female. The only time I get a bit annoyed about it is when I'm with trans people who assume I'm male, mostly because I think, well actually they should know better. There's plenty of people that are genderqueer and genderqueer doesn't have to mean that you look androgynous, it's a different identity.

So for the most part it's when trans people make assumptions about my gender that I get annoyed, rather than a cisgender person seeing me as just male, I don't mind that. I know that sounds a bit of a kind of contradiction but I think for people who should be a bit more open minded, that's why I'm a bit like "stop putting me in a box. I don't want to have a discussion about my gender." That's another reason why I transitioned, because my gender identity is personal to me. I'm happy to talk about it with my partner and my friends, that's a more philosophical point, but it's not a conversation I want to be having with people I don't really know.

I'm in more contact with gay men than I have been for some time. There's quite a culture amongst some gay men to call each other she, and I knew I had kind of made it to the other side when some people started calling me she because they thought I was a gay man. Suddenly for the first time being called she didn't feel painful because it actually meant recognition of the masculinity in me. So I've got to this flip point where actually I quite like being called she sometimes, whether it's because they see me as a gay man or just because of the queering it up a bit.

At FTM Brighton meetings we always say what our preferred pronoun is and I'm quite happy for people to call me whatever. As long as they're being respectful about it, I don't mind if people call me she or it, even, or zie or he. I don't really mind, as long as that respect is there because for me it's not a painful thing anymore. Now that I have that privilege of being seen as he all the time, the sting has been taken out of it.

My gender identity is a little bit complicated I guess. I think what I enjoy most about it is that I just feel the freedom to be however I want to be. So I really like it, for example, when I'm at home with my partner and she's being all butch and I'm just being camp as hell and that feels normal. It's not being affected. It's just I'm expressing my more feminine side, not that necessarily camp is equal to femininity. I guess what I'm trying to say is I feel free to express femininity much more now because it's part of me and it doesn't feel like it's anything forced. So that's what I enjoy about my identity and in coupling with my physical transition is that I have a freedom to express myself however I feel.

Sabah

I know that a lot of queer people of colour in Brighton don't really feel safe about being out and vocal about their identities, our identities, our backgrounds. I think people have just stopped talking about it. The work I'm doing at Allsorts now, is community development, but I'm focusing on BME young people. So essentially it is everything I love doing. I've just started and I'm trying to build a safe space for the BME young people but also making everyone understand why that safe space is necessary.

I'm hoping that we can continue to make Trans Pride a safe space. That's like the most important thing, and I really hope that level of visibility will somehow make people realise that "Oh well, trans people exist and well, I guess they're pretty cool, it's a great party", or something. There was one incident and it was when Bethany Black was on and it was at the end of the day, I think some people who had been drinking in the day came in just to see what was going on, and they were just getting Bethany on stage and just shouting. It wasn't like transphobic it was just, you know, the typical drunken Kemptowners. It was our biggest concern, but the security staff were so great. It was quite nice to do it in a place that was a little park with the gates and stuff. I didn't feel unsafe at any point. It felt so empowering to be surrounded by all these people who aren't even from the trans community who were just walking past, who just came to join in.

The biggest thing is if you ask anyone about trans issues on student campuses, it will be gender-neutral toilets. I think it's so simple just to have male/female toilets and then another toilet, but people who aren't familiar with trans issues don't really understand, and overcomplicate things and then get into their minds like, all these things that trans people are. It is just a fear of the unknown or what's going to happen next. I don't know. It's really funny some of the things people say, but I think when it happens, it's going to, no one will really notice.

Luc

Something that's important to me is being able to use a gender-neutral toilet and so I use the accessible or disability toilets intended for people with mobility issues who may also use a wheelchair. Although I feel justified in having a radar key to use these generally locked spaces, because I have mobility and sensory sensitivity issues with fibromyalgia and/or with Asperger Syndrome, I still feel a bit conspicuous using these toilets in terms of being transgenderqueer. Yet, the 'unisex' nature of the majority of these toilets is invaluable to many trans folk who are transitioning and who can feel justifiably vulnerable to abuse when using the new-to-them 'Gents' and 'Ladies' toilets, especially in the early days of transition before they more easily 'pass' in their chosen gender.

The Brighton & Hove Council's Trans Scrutiny policy decision-making bodies have taken on board the need for there to exist more gender neutral toilets, but this will be a slow process to manifest – just as it's a very slow process to redesign many accessible toilets with the new standard measurements to actually accommodate newer, larger electric wheelchairs.

I'd like to feel more comfortable around more cisgendered guys. I'm an only child and I think I've always wanted to have a brother. I don't know whether that would have made me feel more comfortable in male company or not, but I reckon it would definitely have helped. It's strange, because I obviously look very male, but I get annoyed with myself because, at times, I still feel uncomfortable and doubt myself and how far I've come and how strong I've been.

I go to the gym, I work out, but I still go there and feel, "I don't look like them, I don't look good enough." People sometimes think I'm gay because I'm not some macho alpha male type. It's not a problem that they think I'm gay, but I'd prefer them not to, as I'm not. It is a problem if it's a woman that you like and you're trying to date or attract or whatever, thinks you're gay, or finds it odd that you like different types of music, films et cetera, to what your average guy does. I find that an issue.

Ben

It makes a lot of sense what I'm studying in psychology at the moment. Like we make schemas about everything from a young age and build them up. A schema is a preconceived idea about the world. So, like the example we were given in a lesson was when you go to a restaurant you presume you have an idea of what's going to happen; the waiter comes over to you, shows you to your table, and brings you a menu. And then, if that doesn't happen, you're suddenly left really confused: "Where's the waiter? What table to do I go to?" It's the same with gender. If people are brought up and assume that gender is binary or think like "This is man, man plays rugby, man has short hair. This is woman, woman has long hair, wears dresses, woman has child", that kind of thing, then suddenly there's this person that doesn't fit with that idea, they're assigned male at birth, but takes female pronouns or the other way round. They might be a trans man wearing make-up or a trans woman who wants to keep their facial hair, or whatever. Suddenly people's gender schemas are blown out the water and they don't know how to act.

A lot of the time, when we don't have knowledge of something, human nature is for us to stay away from it, and then it breeds fear of the unknown, then the fear breeds hatred. I guess that's where any phobia comes from. People haven't been brought up to understand it, so then they're going to fear it because it's different. If people are brought up to accept differences and embrace them and learn that everyone is different and that's a good thing, then they're less likely to have these really rigid schemas about things and be more open to people who don't fit the gender binary.

There's the safety issue and the mental issue of just how difficult it is sometimes. Sometimes I don't want to leave the house because I know how people look at me and how people perceive me. It makes me feel horrible, but at the same time, had I not been trans I wouldn't have known a lot of what I know now, and I wouldn't be able to educate other people. Even though that's kind of annoying sometimes, but it's a good thing to be able to spread your knowledge about gender and stuff. I really wouldn't be proactive as I am now. I didn't really know anything about gender minorities at all before researching things.

School is really really ingrained in terms of gender. Thinking back like the changing rooms 'male' and 'female' and separate. It wasn't even that long ago that girls couldn't play football, they could only do netball, and the boys couldn't do netball, they could only do rugby or football. That only stopped like a couple of years before I went to school. There's never any unisex bathrooms, apart from the disabled ones, which I kind of resent having to use. Not that there's anything bad about the connotation of being disabled, but it's like my gender is not a disability to me. It's just another thing, like the same way that I prefer the colour red over pink.

Something I really detest and I've seen it, like it's happened to me. I've seen so many other people kind of follow queer people online and pester them like "What's your gender now?" I'd be like I don't really identify as any. They're like "No, but what is your gender?" I'm like "I don't identify as one." "No, but what is your gender? What's your real name? What genitals do you have? Do you have a dick? Do you have boobs". It's no-one's business, it doesn't matter. If you like a person it doesn't matter whether they have boobs or tentacles coming out of their cheeks. You like the person, whatever. They assume that it's like their business what surgery you've had. It doesn't matter, I am who I am. it's like saying "My favourite colour is green," "Oh you're going to wear everything green now? Are you going to get your skin coloured in green?" No one asks that, it's just ridiculous. I don't see why people have to ask whether I'm going to get a fake dick put on or whether I've grown a dick overnight because that's apparently what happens in cis-people's brains. If you wish hard enough it'll be there.

It's only four years ago a trans woman was murdered in Brighton, but compared to other places it is very safe. Maybe if I was in Russia or Greece or even parts of America, up north in England, not so progressive cities you'd have to decide, is this worth me being unsafe? That's the question, it might be different if I was somewhere else.

One of our tutors used to talk to me about the illusion of gender quite a lot and about how basically he saw that if I passed, I hate that term, but if I was assumed as male by others, then that was because I was tricking them into thinking that was a man when I'm not. He was basically one of those people that believed that you're born a sex and you can change your body, mutilate your body, you can have operations, you can take hormones, but that doesn't ever change what you are. And that really, really bothered me and carried that around with me for ages. That was probably the first time I ever really felt that whole idea of being trapped in your body and the idea of like your body as a cage, or I was born in the wrong body, or whatever the media like to use. I don't think I've ever let go of that, honestly, and it's been more than a year now, and I still haven't.

At uni we talk about the idea that the ultimate privilege is to not know you have privilege. I think that's exactly what cis-privilege is. They have absolutely no idea that they're privileged because they identify as the sex they're assigned at birth, therefore we are so othered it's unbelievable. It's so easy to other anybody you want over anything, hair colour, ginger people, they're othered, for absolutely no reason. It's ridiculous. And race, and ethnicity and nationality, anything you can other anyone for anything. But I think there's greater othering than that from cis-people because they don't even realise they have privilege and I think that's a massive issue

Reuben

Reuben, who lives in Hove with partner Samantha, is a 20 year old Social Science student from Essex. He began his medical transition in 2012 and has recently undergone chest surgery.

Alice

I've got this faith in human nature. I think the people in Russia are only behaving like arse-holes because of what they're told, their upbringing. Given the chance of being nice people, they'd find out straight away, "Oh I feel much more comfortable with this," it would be nice. I don't think kids are born bad. I think they are born okay, and if they're treated with love and respect and so on they'll just get on with it.

I was playing football in the park with my grandsons and there's this kid who joined us and was playing. And after a little while, there was me in my summer dress, kicking the ball around. I was charging around like a big elephant amongst the kids, and this kid was a really good footballer, aged about eleven. He's a friend of my grandson and said, "Excuse me, can I ask you how you know…" and pointed at my grandson.

And I said, "Oh, he's my grandson" and the kid went "Oh, okay" and just got on with it. Obviously they had some inkling that I was slightly different from their mum, or something, but I think kids, given their own opportunities, without being pushed by grown ups telling them things, are accepting.

I can accept when someone makes an odd slip in mis-gendering me, it hurts. I have to tell people, it bloody hurts and I bite my tongue and blink my eyes to stop the tears coming out. I accept it's a mistake, but don't make it that often, please. But, some people just make a thing of "Oh I can't get used to this" you know. "Yes, you can. Yes you can get used to this". I've had comments, when I've not got angry and reacted to it and I've said, "Excuse me, did you say something?" and found they've said something really nice. Like a

chap said something to me the other day, sort of sideways, as if he was making a snide remark. And I trotted up and caught up with him, and said, "Excuse me, I didn't catch that?" And he said, "Oh, I was just saying, I love your shoes" and it was true, he was, and we walked along having a conversation about shoes. He was a lovely man. Now, I could have gone away thinking, "Oh, it's just another one of those derogatory remarks", but I never do now, unless someone very specifically makes a remark.

I hope I don't allow myself to go anywhere near being the victim because the world doesn't want me to be a victim either. Sometimes I think too strong a reaction, creates the reality rather than, even if someone is unpleasant, saying, "Why do you think that? What makes you say that?"

felt desperately lonely and really intimidated by everybody else. I wanted to be really far away from everything in Birkenhead because it was not the most cosmopolitan place in the nineties. We used to get shit every time we went out the front door. My friends and I were the punks and the skaters and then on top of that I was kind of androgynous. I was just really frightened of people and you know, I still am. I'm in my thirties and step out the front door and I'm ready for something. Every time I go out I look everywhere all the time. I'm really aware of what's going on around me, all the time. I'm just getting to grips with having the confidence to feel like I'm out in the world, but just kind of cacking myself about it for a while.

I'm starting to get the confidence to feel like I actually own my space in the world. I want to travel. I want to go everywhere and I spend a good deal of time in not straight places, but not explicitly LGBT spots. I guess mostly to do with the music scene that I like. To go and see bands and playing in bands you have to go to mixed venues. Loads of my dear, dear friends are straight cis-people, who are gorgeous. And there's stuff that they don't necessarily get the same way that myself and my queer friends understand. So I go to queer spaces for that, but it's essential that we, as trans people, get on with our lives in the world. It's ours just as much as it's anybody else's.

This is more of a theory than an opinion I think at this point, but perhaps it's not as bad as we think it is. We carry a lot of self-loathing and a lot of hatred around

with us. And we feel like targets, you know, for abuse and criticism. We feel fragile and we feel vulnerable. I've been thinking about that recently. Is it that bad or is it because we feel that? I'm not saying for a second, that we aren't targets and there aren't people who are going to be arse-holes to us. I'm not that naïve, but I'm trying to reduce how much of my anxiety I ping out into the world. I also think that you could put yourself in a dangerous position if you do that. People see that, and you can make yourself a target if you do that too much. It's a difficult balancing act.

I don't know, it's just the world, not the straight world or the queer world. There are different spaces within it, but it's the world and it's absolutely beautiful. I have wasted quite a lot of time and I don't regret the way I've done things because it was never going to go any differently, was it? But it's the mirror thing. If you be yourself to the world, the world will see who you are. It will treat you like you and you will get nourished by the interactions that you've had.

Maeve

Originally from South Wales, Ludo Foster is a PhD candidate in Gender Studies at the University of Sussex, writing an alternative history of tomboys in popular culture. He's a Siamese cat adoring, Bob Dylan loving vegan fascinated by hidden histories.

Chapter Seven: The whole idea of male-female binary
- I've wiped it out of my head.

Sexuality, intimacy, relationships, finding partners, attraction, dating

I'm most comfortable with the label genderqueer, or androgynous. This is the most authentic 'me' I can explain, and I don't regret the empathy I've inherited along my journey. I feel like I've had many lifetimes in one.

Sexuality and gender are different things, but there is that point where they meet. Like the two lines of an 'X'. That's why I love 'queer' so much, because it's this great umbrella term.

I think even hetero-normative people, cis-people in straight relationships can still identify as queer, and very vehemently as well. I wish people would adopt it more, because I see it as more of an accepting kind of thing. If you label yourself as queer, then it's up to other people to investigate how you identify and what ideals you up-hold. Queer is a being-ness, a sense of self in relation to the mainstream.

In the near future, perhaps we'll discover that everyone exists somewhere on the gender and sexuality spectrum, all spread out. Like CN Lester, I believe this spectrum is more like a constellation, with each of us experiencing the ever increasing variations of passion and identity.

Fox

I believe there's no male or female binary, there's just aspects of gender and maybe a spectrum. It really means that you're just attracted to someone who's somewhere within that spectrum. You may be attracted to people who've got attributes that are more male than female, or the other way round. But it allows you to say "Well okay. I like girls but there's somewhere in that masculine part of the spectrum that I find attractive as well". And so you become more, I guess the word's pansexual.

For me, I did have a moment where I really questioned what was going on and who I found attractive because I never saw myself as a gay man. I puzzled over that quite a bit. As things went on with my transition, I realised that I was probably a bisexual woman. Transitioning opens your eyes to gender and attractiveness and attributes of people. The whole idea of male-female binary – I've wiped it out of my head. That's been a huge benefit to me.

It's best to be upfront because I don't feel like I am trying to fool anyone. If they're honest, a lot of people probably find us attractive. I think I'm attractive. And I think there's more to life than just looks anyway. You know, what's attractive is someone that's just bright and talented and lovely and nice. So the whole idea of whether they're trans or not is not too relevant. It can just make you feel a little bit less confident.

There's always that doubt of how people view you and what they're attracted to. If I knew someone was attracted to me because they think I'm male trying to be a woman I wouldn't like that. I don't think I'd feel comfortable in that relationship. I want people to accept me as a woman but not necessarily in a binary way, it's just that I feel like I was born female, but with male bits.

Michelle

I hate it when people lump together gender and sexuality. Like when you say, "I'm transgender". "Oh you're gay." "No, did you hear what I just said? I said transgender. How does that sound like gay? Did I stutter? No, I didn't." I guess it's just ignorance because a lot of people still conflate trans women, drag queens and effeminate gay men, but it doesn't stop it from being annoying. If people were better educated about transgender people then that probably wouldn't happen.

Ezekiel

Ezekiel, known as Zeke to his friends, is an almost 19 year old trans masculine guy from Brighton (born in the USA). He has plans for testosterone HRT and is about to start studying biochemistry at Kent University.

Ed

Before I transitioned I was not really interested in going out with people, romantic relationships, sexual relationships. I found the whole thing far too daunting and scary. I thought that was just because I was young and naïve and I was somebody who was a bit nervous about getting involved in sex. As the years went on, I realised I couldn't really put it down to that any more. I was, like, "You really need to get over this now". I wasn't like "Oh I don't believe in sex before marriage" and I thought, "Do I hate my body that much that I don't want to have sex with somebody?" It didn't feel like it was that simple. Then what the hell is going on?

It was through trying to understand why I was, at the age of twenty-three, still feeling sex was something awful and how could anybody imagine ever doing

that? I felt like I still had a kind of eight-year-old child's attitude to sex. It was what adults did, and it was all a bit gross and weird. I thought there is something going on here, in my head, that is problematic.

I'd had one boyfriend so I wasn't totally naïve. We were definitely attracted to each other. We'd messed around a bit, but I just went "I just can't do it". It was like a fire went off in my head. And so I needed to figure out what was going on. And it was through writing about my thoughts in my diary that I started to realise there was a gender issue going on. What I clocked first of all was that, whenever I imagined myself in a relationship with somebody, I'd imagine myself as a guy. Even as a child I'd imagined myself as an adult man. And I thought, "That's a bit weird, I'm not sure other women do that". They don't seem to talk about it if they do.

So, then I started looking into wearing more men's clothing and came across the FTM UK website. It was through trying to figure out what the hell was going on with me sexually, and why I had a problem with sex, that I found that I was trans, basically. Then after I started to transition I thought everything would be fine, but it wasn't. I do plan to have surgery and I think that will mostly solve

the problem. My body is just not the thing that is in my head. The mismatch is so profound it's like something screaming in my head and it just needs to be fixed. I can't imagine any way of getting round it other than surgery.

Everything I've tried hasn't worked. I think back to being a teenager and first starting to be aware of attraction and sexual feelings. I was fairly sure as a teenager that I was attracted to women and I think maybe some of my attraction to boys was wanting to be them. I think it was maybe a bit of a muddle of envy and also attraction. So I'm probably attracted to all genders. It seems all the people I've been attracted to have been so different I don't think I could really pin myself down. So that's why I try to avoid giving it as "I'm a pan-sexual", "I'm a bisexual" or "I'm an omni-sexual" because I don't know yet. I think, when I'm ninety-eight and on my death bed, I can look back and then probably I'll have a clearer idea, but even then it's only based on the people I meet during my life. If I'd met different people, I might have looked at it differently. I know I have a sexuality, I think that's probably the most conclusive I can be on the subject. I definitely have one. What it's limited to I don't know, yet.

Rory

It took me until I was about twenty-one to come out properly. That was when I was visiting my sister in Edinburgh. The night before I was meant to come back to Brighton she pinned me against the wall of a nightclub and said, "You're bisexual aren't you?" And I was drunk and said, "yeah, I think so, probably". I fancied her best friend at the time so that probably added to it. So I came back to Brighton and I was, like, "Okay. I'm bisexual now. That means I can have sex with girls". And I ended up having sex with straight men instead which was a bit of a disappointment. Then, on my twenty-first birthday I finally got lucky and met a girl. That was all a bit of a disaster but I thought it was wonderful.

Then I threw myself into being gay for a bit because I soon discovered that you couldn't really be bi as there was just so much biphobia. People wanted to know whether you are straight or gay. So I was, like, I'm going to go gay. And I tried to be a lesbian for a couple of years. My last long-term relationship ended six months before starting testosterone. So I don't think that relationship was affected by trans status. I had a couple of girlfriends when I started taking T and they were just disasters. Now I'm in another long-term

happy relationship and most of the time my girlfriend forgets I'm trans. Sometimes she has a little bit of a shock when we have sex and she's, like, "Oh yeah, that isn't there is it?" But I've been quite lucky in dating and relationships because I've been part of the queer community. Everyone's known me as being trans and I've been just socialising around the kind of people that don't really care about trans in that way.

I think all my recent lovers have preferred the fact that I don't have certain bits of anatomy. I had a girlfriend that was a bit transphobic, didn't really get it and said some quite hurtful things. Needless to say that relationship didn't last but it's not really been an issue for me. My sexuality is queer as well so that's always given scope for liking all kinds of people regardless of their gender. And liking all kinds of activity regardless of the bodies. Certainly my interest in sex has changed, it has increased with testosterone and I think when you've got more interest in sex you start exploring different ways of having sex or different things about sex. At times I'm more attracted to men and at times I'm more attracted to women, that's not really changed.

I've always been an open-minded person and totally accepting of all kinds of people. I used to wish that I was gay and I'd hang out with gay people. When I first came out, I came out as gay because that's what made the most sense. I am attracted to fellas but I was attracted to women as well. I thought maybe I think I'm attracted to women because that's a safe bet, and I'm just frightened of men because most of the people who have ever been shit-heads to me have been men.

It wasn't 'til around the time I came out that I met a guy who was older that me, who identified as gay, who started telling me that he'd been to all this queer stuff. And I found out what queer was, and activism and this whole punk stuff that was totally aside from the gay scene. He really enlightened me to all that. I'd seen Queer as Folk and I thought, "This is going to be like this Holy Grail place where everyone's going to be all natural, and have this really warm, loving northern manner. And I'd be taken under their wing and have adventures and fall in love". So I met this guy and he enlightened me and I started to think, "Well, maybe I legitimately could be bisexual".

So, I tried to be gay, that didn't work, because I fell for this woman immediately. We started this love affair that was off and on for ten years and that was like, obviously I'm not gay. And I got my first boyfriend and we were together for two or three years and I really loved him, but I always felt we were on slightly different pages about our connection. I think he's changed how he identifies now, but this is ten years down the line, and we're friends again. I did drive myself kind of round the bend with it but started to transition in my way.

I grew my hair and started to wear make up again, and got back in this relationship with the woman that I'd got with when I came out of the closet. We moved in together and she was sort of supportive in this "I like androgynous boys" kind of way. So she liked my presentation but wasn't down with me actually being a chick. That became really damaging and she said some stuff that really hurt me. "You're not a woman, you'll never be a woman. You've no idea what it's like"; that kind of stuff. It broke my heart and made me furious and I left and couldn't explain to her why it wasn't working because she wouldn't listen. I packed up and left her a note, and it was like "This isn't working, I'm outta here". We've been off and on together since, but that summer I cut my hair and I stopped wearing make up and I thought "Well, this hurts too much, fuck it."

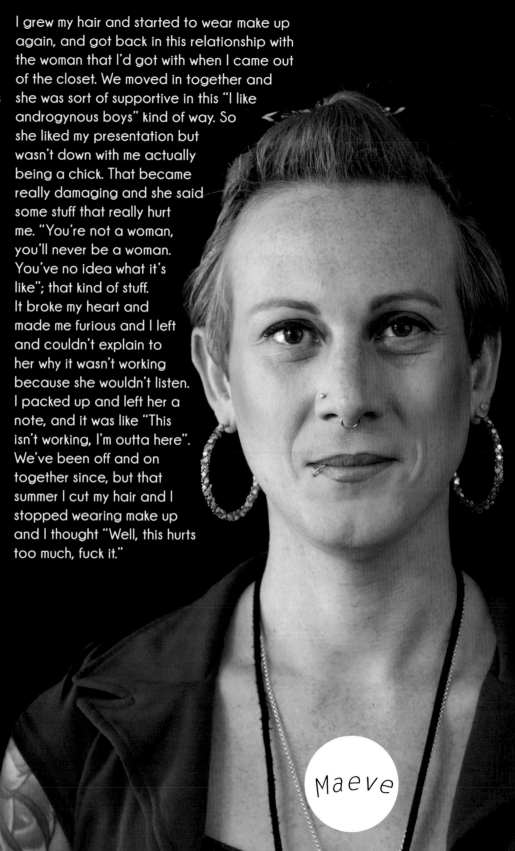

Maeve

Sabah

Cass

I didn't really take myself too seriously when I was in Brighton as a lesbian. When you're at university there are great lesbian nights every week and all these societies and events. So I lost myself for a bit. I wasn't really doing too well at university. I took a year out and I still can't believe that I spent one year just going out and making loads of friends and meeting loads of girls and drinking too much. By the time I got hold of myself again, I met someone who was really, really important to me and she was one of the NUS officers. She was an activist at heart. I don't even know how I came out to her because it was something that we just spoke about. It was like she just gave me the space to explore and we used to talk about things. And then suddenly it'll be "Oh, like that's feminism".

I then started to see things from a different perspective and got involved in politics. I was just automatically bored when I heard politics being spoken about before, but I think it was just about finding the right angle to explore it with. I was with her when I transitioned and I became myself. I was with her for two years and then it wasn't working out, and I just had to continue on my journey.

I was seeing a guy the year before last. It was really sweet. It was good. He was quite posh and quite well off and his attitude was "I like boys, I like girls, and I like everything in between, and I don't care who knows". He was the first guy I'd met who wasn't embarrassed by me, or wasn't uncomfortable. We didn't have to find some secret pub to go to. Because so many of the guys are so insecure, so worried. People call them "tranny chasers", it's so horrible. But lots of them are quite sweet guys and they just generally like us. But then a lot of them are quite creepy. He was quite straightforward because he had this libertarian, laid back attitude to sexuality and sex, and I know I wasn't the only person he had in his life. He moved on.

I never had considered myself to prefer men over women, I'd like both. But hormones have changed that quite a lot. It's definitely men for me now. I still appreciate women but it's not sexual at all any more. So it's a tricky one because heterosexual men tend to be quite narrow-minded generally. Not all of them, I know plenty that aren't but, yeah, especially when it comes to who they sleep with.

Gloria

I think I struggle with not only my gender issues but also my sexuality. For most of my life, between my twenties and my late thirties, gender issues would always pop up whenever I was in a relationship. It would always cause me problems at which point the pressures from that would start to affect the relationship as well. So most of my relationships weren't really that successful. I think principally because they were always the woman I wanted to be and I would always put them on a pedestal. They had the body I wanted, they had the life I wanted, everything about them. And in the end it would kill the relationship.

For a long time I thought I might have been gay because I didn't realise in my late teens, early twenties, that gender dysphoria existed and that I wasn't on my own. There were other people in the world like me. There wasn't much information around and there was nowhere to go to discuss it. It seems stupid nowadays, in the twenty-first century, to think that, but we are talking about over thirty years ago. Things were very different in those days. I did struggle with my sexuality. I did experiment. I did have relationships with men as well but it really wasn't for me. So, in the end, my last relationship came to an end in the late nineties, and I didn't engage in another because I was too busy resolving my gender dysphoria.

At the time I was spending a lot of time working overseas. I still lived in the area but I did spend a lot of time bouncing backwards and forwards. That came to an end in 2001. I stopped the travelling. Mainly because I was nearly forty and hadn't any friends. I hadn't got a life other than work. I needed to get my life back on an even keel. As I did that, my gender dysphoria got worse but I had time to think about it more, to decide what I wanted for the rest of my life. So in 2005 I decided I was going to transition.

...don't know that the fact that I've been on a unfixed journey with my sexuality has been solely to do with my being trans. I've always been interested in men, but my long-term partners have always been women and in this way I'm straight. Except that I'm so not straight, I'm one of them crazy queers people talk about. I think being with men post-transition filled a yearning for a deeper understanding of male physicality, and intimacy brought that with it. I wanted to touch and hold and see men's bodies. I've never been taught by my father how to be a man. There was so much intimate knowledge missing. I think I wanted to transfer a bit of the experience over as well, in so far as I wanted to see fully functioning sexual male bodies and imagine myself in that space. I think the way I explored the journey of physicality can be traced to understanding my own trans body, what I could and couldn't cope with and what I desired. My sexuality embodies my physical theatricality.

I'm in a very happy and dynamic long-term relationship with my girlfriend, who's the most supportive person of me in the world. I'm so very lucky to have such an open-minded person in my life. She's never been with a trans person before and previously she was in a very long-term relationship with a cisgendered male. So I had a lot of hang-ups when I got with

her, about whether or not we were going to have a sexually fulfilled partnership, because she'd been with a cisgendered guy for years. But she maintains that my body is of absolutely no consequence to her, it's about what's on the inside. That might be a bit of a cliché, but she always eventually gives in when I nag her enough and tells me that she fancies me.

My girlfriend and I are currently in the process of securing a sperm donor. My partner wants to go through the physicality of having a baby and then we'll adopt after that. But I don't want to know the donor. I've decided that that would threaten my masculinity, and my security in the role as father, even though I honestly know it shouldn't. Sometimes you can't rule your heart with your head. So we're going to go for

an anonymous donor and then, when our child is old enough, obviously they will have the legal right to find out what they want to about their biological ancestry. But I'm secure in that. By the time eighteen years have passed, I will have had the role of father for long enough to be very happy for them to find out what they need to and still be confident that I am daddy.

E - J

On some contact information – or equality and diversity – forms I'm very excited when there is an 'other gender' tick box and there's usually a line: 'please state' and I can put down any number of my trans identities texts that I want; but that's still not common and they quite often just ask if you're male/female. In terms of ethnicity, as white and British – with a quarter Irish – I do not have a need to create acceptance regarding my race, nor do I feel this need with creed as I'm more into Gnostic spirituality than religion. But I do tick boxes for having mental health, neuro-behavioural and physical disability issues. And I will probably tick a box of 'other' under sexuality and write 'Asexuality' as that does not come up as an option. However, asexual implies a choice to not be genitally sexual with another, but it doesn't make reference to who I might want to be a romantic partner with: whether that's a pan-sexual choice that includes being with a trans person, or whether that's about being a gay trans-masculine person.

I guess I'm politicising the fact that asexuality exists in our highly sexed-up society, so I tick that box and write it just to increase awareness. It's not that sex doesn't interest me at all: it's the complexity of it; I think that reflects relating difficulties for me as an Aspie person. There's part of me that feels that now, having transitioned, I could only be with a person who was either born intersex or who identifies as genderqueer, in that they would have some understanding of what I'd gone through, but I really don't want to put up those limitations. I might fall in love with a cisgendered woman again; I really don't know.

Luc

I identify as a trans man and I also relate very much as well to a gender queer kind of identity, but very much on that trans-masculine spectrum. Ultimately I suppose it's been a process which has gone along, as well, with my coming out as trans. I feel strongly that gender is very much the spectrum and I've never really gone much towards a binary kind of identity. I've never felt strongly female. I always very much felt I've gone more towards male, but am very comfortable in that kind of fluid position really. I'm very comfortable with masculinity, in its many forms.

I'm thirty-eight years old, so I wasn't brought up at a time when we would hear a lot about these things. It was very much male or female and there were no real choices. So, since discovering these things, it's been really interesting to explore them and to realise what a spectrum there is, and that there is a place for so many different forms of femininity or masculinity. So, for me it's a constant fluid learning space, my gender identity. And even though I feel very much male I'm also very comfortable with some of the female socialisation I've had. That's opened up a female dimension as well within me, in the way of communication, and maybe the way I can connect to people emotionally. So that is a good fit for me. That's my relation to genderqueer.

Ludo

Ben

One thing that has been a big surprise for me in becoming part of the trans community is that I now feel I'm a bit like the only 'straight in the village' most of the time. Because I guess I always thought, once I became part of the trans community with other trans guys, that most trans guys would be straight and just be attracted to women. So obviously my eyes have been very much opened getting to know people in the queer community and realising that it's not one set pathway when you're a trans guy or a trans woman. I do feel that sometimes I'd like to know more straight trans guys, but the problem is that a lot of straight trans guys make the transition and then disappear/go stealth. Maybe they're part of the community while they're transitioning and then they go and live their life and obviously they're not open about it, they're stealth. They don't want people to know, so it's very hard to really get to know any other guys like that.

I find it difficult because it's only been in the last few months I've been more open to meeting women who identify as bisexual, as well as straight women. I mean I am more open to meeting a woman if she identifies herself as queer. I think in the past I was always worried that they wanted me for the wrong reason. Maybe they wanted me because of looking slightly feminine in some way, or having quite feminine characteristics or

whatever. As I become more confident in myself, it's not so much of a problem now, but it affects me all the time.

In my long-term relationship, I met my partner then online, soon after I'd graduated in 2003. She was straight, she is straight as far as I know still. So, when I got to know her online I'd already transitioned. I'd changed my name. I hadn't had any surgery yet, I'd been on testosterone for about two years by then, and I did worry. She didn't live where I lived, so we were communicating online about a month or two before we met up. I was just really worried that once we met she'd instantly know about me being trans. I don't think she would have done, but I was just paranoid about it. So I told her the night before we were going to meet in London and I just thought she'd turn around and say "Oh forget it then, I don't want to know", but she was fine about it. She said she always knew there was something I wasn't telling her. It was a big thing for her to get her head round because she'd never been with a trans guy. She'd never really had anything to do with the LGBT community. It's only now I look back and realise how understanding she was.

This year I've been dating a lot more, which has been a lot of fun, but it's also been quite traumatic. If the woman hasn't known about it beforehand and was straight, and I'd just met her, say, online or in a bar or through a friend or whatever, I still have that problem of having to explain stuff because of surgery-related issues. It's something that I have explain to them and either I have to make something up and not talk about the trans stuff, or just come out with the trans stuff. I'm only happy to start talking about that if I feel the relationship's going somewhere, but obviously not in a one night stand situation. It's very difficult and I did have a very uncomfortable situation a couple of months ago where someone questioned me about it, in the middle of everything. She didn't chuck me or anything, but obviously it was very uncomfortable and it knocked my confidence a lot. So I'm hoping, once it's all completed, it won't be an issue, but at the moment it's always a real stumbling block for me.

I watched a documentary the other day and it was this couple consisting of a trans guy and a trans woman. And this trans woman was talking, and her mum was there. Her mum was saying "Oh yeah, when Katie was little she used to hold her penis and tell me that she didn't want it. And then I told her dad 'Oh, you know, you'd better get ready for having a gay son". And I was, like, does not wanting your penis mean you're gay? Because if you're attracted to other male people then that doesn't mean you're not male. I was so confused at that. But I think it's just because people are so obsessed about categorising people that it becomes that. It's something that really needs education. Like being trans and being gay, or being anything, is not the same thing. You can be trans and gay, whoo.

My girlfriend makes me happy. When I say to her "Do I look like a man today?" she says "You always look like a man. Stop asking me this question. You always, always look like a man. Stop worrying, you don't have to worry". And she always says to me "What do I have to say for you to believe me?" And I'm always, like, "There's nothing that you can say". Then she says "Well, I'll just keep telling you then". My girlfriend is probably the first person I've been really close to where I just don't need to explain anything ever. I never had to say to her, like, "Oh, when I'm getting dressed, or when I'm doing this, can you not do this. Or can you not say this to me". She just knows and I think that's important. I think eventually everyone's going to be like that and you won't need to explain anything to anybody because they'll already know.

Reuben

I've been with my girlfriend Rosa for over thirteen years now. I still can't believe she's been with me after all this time, especially as we were so young when we got together. She's been extremely supportive since day one and that has made this journey so much easier. In some ways I wish she would have met me now and not seen some of the sides of me I would rather forget. I know that my dysphoria has had a huge effect on our relationship over the years and sometimes I wish I could erase all of that. But when I really think about it, I don't know what I'd have done without her through that time and it has made our relationship a lot stronger. Things have improved drastically since medically transitioning. I'm just happier within myself and that naturally extends to everyone around you but I'm still in this awful self absorbed stage, it's all "me, me, me" all the time and I do neglect our relationship. She's always been there, the thought of not having her in my life scares me more than anything.

Testosterone and top surgery has made me way more comfortable with myself, but even being with my long term partner who totally gets me and sees me as male is difficult with my high dysphoria. I'm not sure I'd cope very well trying to date while trans, in terms of disclosing and my feelings of people not seeing me as a "real man".

Darcy

E-J is a fashion historian and curator of dress, specialising in late Victorian haute couture. His ambition is to establish a Museum of Transology, an exploration of trans people's lives through dress and objects.

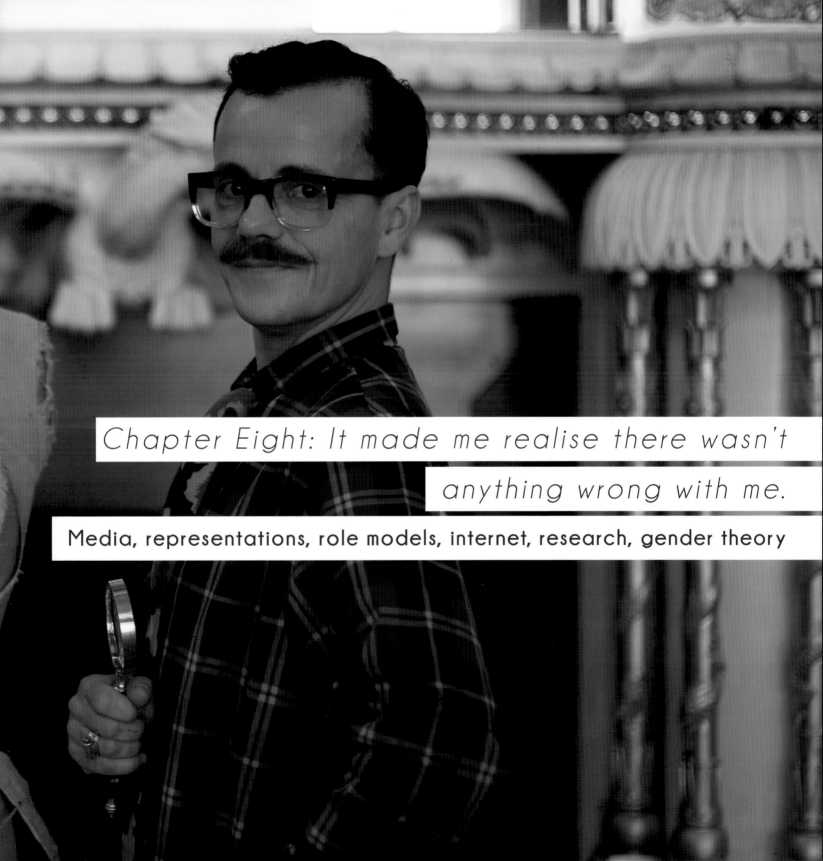

Chapter Eight: *It made me realise there wasn't anything wrong with me.*

Media, representations, role models, internet, research, gender theory

Sabah

I feel like I already knew who I was going to be when I was really young, maybe five or something. I was watching a documentary in my parents' room about someone who was going through a sex change and sex reassignment. This person had a hormone injection of testosterone and they were doing these tests and talking about it. For some reason I completely understood it. I was like "Oh my god. You can have a sex change." There's a real taboo around effeminate men. There's a documentary called Pakistan's Hidden Third Gender and it's about a community called Hijras who are trans women. But they've been ostracised from the rest of the community. The only work they can get is either as sex workers or dancing and entertaining at weddings. Even then they're expected to perform sex acts. It's somehow okay because it's a man dressed up as a woman, in their eyes. It's really complicated and quite dark. It makes me kind of uneasy.

In the media, people will talk about if someone's gay and talk about that in a respectful way and understand that gay rights are still something to fight for. But in terms of trans history and how we've always been there and respecting our journeys and our experiences, people still don't really understand. We're still fighting for that and sometimes it's a battle that we lose. Also, I was looking at 'before and after' photos thinking "Oh, does it work? What am I going to look like?" and there was always something missing. Then I realised that everyone I'm looking at is white. How am I going to know how this affects me? It made me really think about how I need to find that support.

There aren't enough role models in the UK, and that really does make a difference. When you look up celebrities and Hollywood it's like they're not even real people. But Laverne Cox, she's really paving the way for a lot of trans actresses and actors and she's really speaking out about it. Even having a trans person cast to be a trans character was really important. There are so many important people here in Brighton and London as well, I think people don't give themselves enough credit, you know, it's role models who are really stars.

Ludo

It's changing time. Things have changed for trans people. In my life-time I've seen a lot of changes from my own experience in that there was a great invisibility of the trans experience in popular culture, mainstream culture. It's because we've had people like Professor Stephen Whittle, to name but one person. And in a contemporary sense we've got people like C N Lester, and Paris Lees, and in a global sense, people like Laverne Cox and Janet Mock: trans women, American trans women and activists. It's slow and it's going to take legislation, especially when it comes to the attitudes to how people are treated in a medical sense, but I think as people start to speak out and become more empowered, visibility is happening, really slowly, but it is happening.

More positive and more nuanced and diverse representations are happening, really slowly. It's a little too slow, in a way, because you can feel, as a trans person, that you are a little ahead of your time sometimes. You can see how things could change, how things could be different, but it just doesn't seem to be happening.

Laws are still a little bit behind. For instance there's issues with toilets and bathrooms and passports and all kinds of legal kind of things that are really important. Being transgender is still seen as a mental health issue. One of the big changes could be how gender nonconforming children are viewed and treated and understood. There needs to be a lack of stigma and shame and an understanding as well. I'm kind of an optimist I suppose, so I am hoping that these things will happen. It's fundamental that the most marginalised in any community need to be the most elevated and appreciated and respected. I would like to think there'd be a time when we wouldn't need to have a Trans Day of Remembrance.

vaguely knew about April Ashley), and people would refer to a bloke having changed into a woman. I ached for it. I remember reading when I was a kid about somebody who had been a big sports star in America who had decided to be a woman. That's how it was put. And I remember feeling really, really envious and thinking, "I can't do that, how can I do that? I'm not in America, I'm not famous, I'm just little and nobody". It was getting really bad. I was really depressed, more and more depressed. And there was a programme on the telly about Paddington Green, and there was a girl on there called Jackie, who I had a huge empathy with and I found afterwards, lots of other people in the general population had a great empathy and sympathy for. At the same time, programmes like Ten Years Younger came out, where there was something about you that you could get rid of. Facial hair, that was a big thing. I thought, "If I do anything. I'd be a bearded woman and that's not what I want". But then they showed this laser thing and I thought, "Oh, maybe". It was just these little chinks of hopes that you could do something about yourself.

So, I started going to get laser treatment for my facial hair. Then there was a big hiatus when my ex got ill, so I looked after her for a long while and I had to hide it all again. I couldn't go. Then it got too much and I did go and carry on with the treatment – not that it bloody worked. I just got more and more desperate. Luckily there was the internet. You can look on the internet and find out there's such things as people who are transgender. You find that there are organisations. I tried several and eventually I got the phone number of the Switchboard in Brighton. That's how I ended up in Brighton really. Switchboard, The Clare Project, coming over to that.

People give you such conflicting advice and sometimes people say things as if they're in the know. There's some people, quite famous people who have written books that I find quite insulting to transgender people and they speak for transgender people. They don't blooming speak for me and never did. Who am I to give advice – but the advice I would give is be true to yourself as much as you can, as soon as you can and that line, it's become corny now, but I love it, "Don't be afraid and don't be ashamed to make your own world".

Alice

I remember when I was a kid, maybe a teenager, seeing a documentary on BBC Spotlight, about a trans woman who was a bus driver near Exeter and being quite fascinated by that. Clearly she was having a really hard time. A lot of my mates were gay or bi or lesbian and my mum's gay so I enjoyed a pink enclave where I was living at the time. I remember my best friend, when I was sixteen, expressing trans feelings and wanting to explore being a woman and I was actually a little transphobic back then and I said, "No, no, this is madness, don't do it". It's really ironic that ten years later I go back and see him and he's still he and I'm now he when I was she.

The TransFabulous arts festival in London really stuck in my mind as a formative experience. It was quite a pivotal point for me. I remember seeing this guy who was an acrobat. He was just doing these amazing things with his body. Lifting himself up with his little finger and you could see every muscle in his body and he was just wearing pants. Not only was he just amazing with his body but you are also thinking "Oh my god you're FTM. You've had all your surgery. You can't tell". And not only that, but "You're now performing half naked with the most amazing body that you've toned every single muscle of. You have this amazing strength". And realising that actually if I was so inclined and trained as hard as he probably did (which is never going to happen), there's still that potential that I could do that with my body. So it made me think further out of the box.

It's quite easy for us to think that we've been dealt a really bad set of cards about our bodies. We're never going to achieve stuff with them and for whatever reason we don't. Maybe it's because we can't be bothered, maybe we're not quite built that way. The point is that it's not the gender issue that's the reason why we can't do these things.

Rory

It was whilst I was at university that I first realised that my issues with gender were not peculiar to me. I saw a television programme, I think it was 1981 or 1982, and there was a documentary about a male-to-female transsexual. The moment I saw that programme, I knew exactly what my issues were. It felt like a great relief. Like a weight had been lifted off my shoulders, because for a long time, as a teenager, and into my late teens, I felt like there was something wrong with me; like I was ill, like I had mental health problems. And when I saw that programme it twigged for me.

I was not able to discuss my situation with anybody. We weren't encouraged in our family to be particularly open about sexuality or gender or anything like that unfortunately. We are talking about over thirty years ago. Life's very different now, but in those days very few people knew about anything like that. Gender dysphoria was not a very well known issue. Access to information was very limited. You had the library and documentaries on the telly. There were research papers and books written by people, even then. But my guess is that the local public library would probably not have those books and they wouldn't be on the book list either, because they might be deemed to have been subversive or inappropriate. We are talking about a time when it was still fairly uncommon to be anything other than the gender you were born with and the sexuality that most people considered to go with that gender and anybody else was considered to be abhorrent.

It made me realise that there wasn't anything wrong with me, that it wasn't abnormal for me to feel that way. But it also made me realise that I wasn't going to be able to do anything about it, because there were no facilities or services provided for me to deal with it, with any help from anybody. So I realised of course that things were not going to change in society and that I just had to carry on hiding, being somebody I wasn't. When the internet became easily accessible, I spent a lot of time in the early 2000s just researching it, finding out whether it was still being dealt with. To my surprise, there was lots of information available. I looked at all of it and thought I've got to do it, I have to, at forty-one years old. I can't spend the next half of my life being as unhappy as I have spent the first of my life. It's stupid.

Gloria

Ed

More people are coming out younger. I don't know why. Is it all to do with Hayley Cropper? It doesn't seem likely. She was a trans woman in Coronation Street, but she's been that character for like twenty years. Whenever I complain, or other people complain about lack of trans representation in the media, people always go, "But what about Hayley Cropper?" One lone cisgender actress trying to hold together the trans representation in the media all on her own and then she dies. Being part of a transgender Yahoo group gave me loads of information. I read Stephen Whittle's White Book, and it scared the life out of me. It said things like "When you go to your first appointment with a psychiatrist you have to wear a suit, otherwise you won't be taken seriously". And it was probably about twenty years out of date by the time I read it. I started reading a few books. I read Jamison Green's book, I read Just Add Hormones and a book by Riki Anne Wilchins, and it was a real muddle of information – lot of bleak stories. A lot of political identities and the importance of deconstructing gender as if that was what trans people had to do. I found that really overwhelming.

Loren Cameron's Body Alchemy was really a relief, because here was just a bunch of pictures of people, looking like guys, who I knew must have at some point looked like just a bunch of women. So that was just like "Oh it works. Oh that's great" They had pictures of surgery, which also blew my mind. And they had two or three paragraphs of information about their lives. "I was unhappy, I didn't know why", "I'm a motorbike mechanic", "I'm a doctor", "I've got a partner", "I've got kids", "I'm bi", "I'm straight" and it made me think, "God, these are just people, that's fine. I'll probably fit in. Clearly whatever I want to do will be okay".

Probably from that point on I figured I'm not going to let myself be swayed by the 'right' trans thing to do. I think Loren Cameron's book really did just make me think, I can do it how I like now. This is my thing, nobody else can tell me. It was quite interesting, because trans stuff was still so new, both to me and largely to the world, it felt like I could do anything I liked with it, there was no prescribed what trans-ness was. I could invent it for myself.

Ruth

You have to deal with the press in a particular way and expect them to exaggerate things, I've had a dose of that myself. I did an article for a small women's magazine that people pick up and read before they go off to bingo on a Thursday morning. I had full editorial control and it came out as a nice article. That was in February a year or so ago, and nothing more went on. Then the reporter who'd done the interview with me sold the article. He rang me up and said, "Well, The Sun's interested in you, would you like to?" And I said, "Well, let them pay a bit for me, you know," so they paid a bit. Anyway, that was all right, but of course the next day I was headlines in The Sun as the oldest transgender person in the country. The day after I was on Daybreak Television and I was on BBC in the evening programme nationally and all sorts of places.

Of course the next thing that happens is that, without anyone having disclosed my address, there are people knocking at my door from all the women's magazines, the salacious ones. They were doing a bidding war and it started with £1000 and it went to £2000, then £3000 and in the end I had an offer, I think of £5000 for an article. I turned every one of them down, because the more they pay, the more they want, and they would want the whole of my family to be dragged into the spotlight regardless of their own privacy.

When I've appeared in newspapers, I've always insisted on having a lot of editorial control. Last year I did a two-page article on the women's page of the Daily Mail and was quite happy to do so and they co-operated beautifully. But the media can pick on anyone that happens to be in the wrong place at the wrong time, and make a ridiculous situation about it. It's very, very difficult to stop them doing that because what they're after is readership and sensation and it's only somebody with the right force of character who can keep them in check. If they get some unfortunate person in an unfortunate situation they'll have them absolutely flayed alive and hung up to dry for everyone to see. And I'm afraid it happens.

Maybe in a few years time it won't matter. I've come across people who want desperately to do some sort of documentary about me being transgendered, and I've said, "That's not the issue. You've seen them on television three or four times a year, again and again, it's not news any more". This is hackneyed, it's gone full circle, it's gone too far and so now nobody's bothered. It's not a point of ridicule any more.

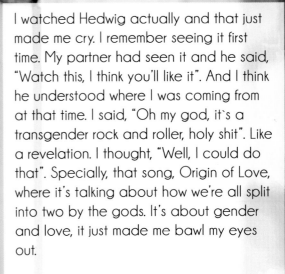

I watched Hedwig actually and that just made me cry. I remember seeing it first time. My partner had seen it and he said, "Watch this, I think you'll like it". And I think he understood where I was coming from at that time. I said, "Oh my god, it`s a transgender rock and roller, holy shit". Like a revelation. I thought, "Well, I could do that". Specially, that song, Origin of Love, where it's talking about how we're all split into two by the gods. It's about gender and love, it just made me bawl my eyes out.

When I went back to university I ended up living in this tiny little room that you could nearly touch the walls either side with your hands. I was living with Juliet Jacques. I met her just before she started her transition, which was really inspiring, because she knew I was thinking about it, and we really spurred each other on. One day there was a little knock on the door, and I hear "Hello?" I open the door, and she says "I've burnt all my man clothes and now I haven't got any clothes." and I fell about. "I've burnt them all and now I don't have any clothes, what am I going to do?" But, that was ace, that was really inspiring.

After coming out about my transition I did a big cry with my mum and we had dinner at a restaurant. Then we came back home and I said, "If this hasn't been too much of a brain challenge so far, do you mind if I show you some stuff?" And she said, "No, of course". So, I showed her the My Genderation video of Alice Denny. And while she was watching, the penny really dropped. And she said, "I get this. It's good isn't it?"

Maeve

Sarah

I was on a Channel Four documentary series called My Transsexual Summer, back when I was trying to move to England to begin my transition. I'd sent Channel Four an email because they were asking for help with some research. They got back in touch with me. I said, "I'm coming to live in England. I intend on starting my transition", and they said, "All right then, we'll meet you off the boat". They followed me the first three or four months of transition and living as female. Something like 5.5 million people watched the series when it premièred, and it's been syndicated in god knows how many countries, worldwide. From Sweden to Israel to Australia, to Canada, all around the world.

There was a huge element of me owning my own story. When I was back in Jersey I didn't want to be known as 'that transsexual'. I wanted an element of control over how other people perceived me. On the documentary, although I didn't have as much control as I wanted to, I could set the narrative. Although none of it was acted, I knew that I could carry myself with a little bit of dignity as much as I could. I knew that it would be sympathetic to trans people in general. I spent a lot of time with the producers and the camera people, they gained my trust. I'm really glad I did it, it's changed my life completely, although it's still weird getting used to people recognising me on the bus.

My friends in Jersey call me a celebrity, and I'm not. I took part in a documentary series. I didn't take part in the X Factor or some get famous quick type shows. I took part in this show because I remember seeing other TV shows about trans people in the past and I remember the hope that that gave me, the knowledge that I was not alone, I wanted to have that opportunity to have that effect on someone else. I thought that they showed me to be much more of a goody two shoes than I thought I was. I was quite happy with it actually. I think they showed me to be a little bit more shy than I am. But, you know, at the time it was literally day one of living as female they were filming, so there was a huge element of being unsure about myself. I was lacking in confidence and that was what the whole summer was about for me, it was growing in confidence.

I'll tell you what my favourite experience was at Trans Pride. It had just stopped raining and I was sitting around the corner having a quiet beer and this parent walked up to me with a little six year old child, and they said, "Oh, you're Sarah, aren't you?" We got chatting and it turned out this kid was completely obsessed with My Transsexual Summer. They were just so happy to be at Trans Pride and everything was amazing. I went over and introduced them to Fox and to Karen, who were both on the show as well. I think we made this kid's week. Just seeing that joy and having that kind of effect on somebody, is why I do everything that I do. It's so important to be visible, because you can have that effect just by being visible. You don't have to do anything other than be yourself.

Fox

Even though I was on that documentary which was watched by 5.5 million people, it's easy to just go out and live my life. I think I have that passing privilege now but it wasn't always the case. I take great satisfaction in just being able to go about my life and it's not a huge deal. I get more homophobic abuse if people assume I'm a gay man.

'People who do know that I'm trans - maybe they've watched something about me - feel more connected because they know more about me. I've been quite an open book so they feel close already and feel safe to tell me their own experiences, or a story about how their children are trans or they know someone else who's trans. Or how they watched My Transsexual Summer and they didn't understand before, but then all of a sudden everything clicked into place. It felt like it was the right thing to do, to put myself 'out there' for trans awareness.

I thoroughly encourage everyone to stand up and tell their stories. Hopefully, in five, ten years time, it's going to be a complete non-issue. It's just another flavour of being human. I think we're progressing. Before I transitioned, I remember meeting a guy called Amos Mac and I was like "Wow. I didn't realise that you could transition and be fashionable as well". It just exploded my mind. I don't know why, it was such a basic thing.

Regardless of who you are, it's not like you turn into a different person post-transition. If you're shy before hand you're going to be shy afterwards. And there was this new wave of trans people who were transitioning and it seemed less heavy and less difficult and more like you could integrate. I just started to see things as being more possible.

I noticed what seemed to be missing from the trans communities. We are living in an electronic age, and trans groups are accessible via Facebook. But what I found was that all the trans groups I saw were very much talking about the news and regurgitating news stories about people being mean to trans people, and there was very little actual trans support going on. Everything that was coming out was negative, so people were saturated with negative news. So I formed my own group, called Transiness. I made it a positive space and said, "Look if you want to post things, post them, but make them all positive. About your achievements as a trans person. About any positive trans news. Just so that you can feel nice about yourself". And it's taken off.

It's lovely to hear people's stories about how they're transitioning and their little successes. I talk online on various groups, to trans people from across the world of all types of ages. And one thing I discovered was that trans people have a massive capacity to be able to heal each other, just through talking with each other. Because what we all seem to share is that we'd held that secrecy for so long and we've been trained like that. To talk with other trans people, trans men as well, but mainly trans women, it's cathartic and it's so helpful.

I wish I'd known some trans people before I transitioned. For people who are considering what transitioning means for them and who they want to be and who they can be, it's vital those of us who can and who are brave enough to come out and say we do exist, stand up as role models and friends. The ageing trans population that has not accessed medical treatment is probably bigger than the ageing trans population who have. So, it's a matter of us getting our faces out and going "This is a place you can drop in, this is a place where you can meet people. This is a place where you can talk about how your partners are coping, how your parents are coping, how your kids are coping, how you're coping." I desperately wish I'd had that.

Rebecca

E-J

Judith Butler says that gender is performative. It's like you perform a gender, and regardless as to whether you want to perform gender or not, everybody does in absolutely everything they do. And sometimes people get scared when they see people who perform gender in ways that they've never seen before. So the idea of a trans guy wearing make-up or a trans woman performing in drag shows, people find that really difficult because they have never seen a person that fits into that sort of category before. It completely changes the way that they see gender and therefore in a sense jeopardises the way they read the world as well, because everything is gendered.

So, as soon as somebody pulls away from that, are visibly queer, identify as queer or are trans, then that's sometimes really difficult for people to get their heads round. I think it's very difficult to break away from any category that you've identified as for however long. And equally I think it's the same with gender. Even though I identify as a man quite strongly, I have a few things about myself that I really like and that happen to be quite feminine attributes as well.

Just because somebody is transgendered or transsexual or whatever, it doesn't mean that they haven't been socialised in the same way as someone who is not trans, into thinking that gender is binary. If you're a man then you have short hair and you don't wear make-up. And if you're a woman you have long hair and you do wear make-up. Trans people aren't exempt from that. I think that's where hyper-feminine trans women or the hyper-masculine trans man, ideals come from. Because like the cis-community, the wider community, everybody, is so much more comfortable with you if you fit in a box. I think cis-men wearing make-up but still identifying as a man, it fits into a box better than a trans man who wears make-up. Trans people aren't exempt from the idea of gender or what the gender ideals are. Hegemonic masculinity, hegemonic femininity, it still exists for trans people as well.

Reuben

Edward has lived in Brighton since 2010 and volunteers with FTMB, a transmasculine support group, MindOut and LGBT HIP. He's studying for a degree in psychology.

Chapter Nine: I can see a future now and it's a future that I want to be part of.

Hope, generational differences, fulfilment, work, creativity

I feel like I'm actually just ready to start life now. Not to discredit anything that I've done because I've had a full life so far in the thirty-four years that I've been knocking around on this planet, it's been fun and I've done good stuff. I've met some amazing people and I've contributed to the world and made things, so it's not been a waste – but I can see a future now and it's a future that I want to be part of. All that buzzing static anxiety and self-loathing is just melting away from me now and things are aligning. So many good things and interesting things have happened for me since I decided to just kind of be myself. The work that I do is getting more interesting, and more opportunities have come up. It's because of this two-way process where, if you be yourself people can see who you are and you get stuff back off them and then they get stuff from you. So, now I feel like I'm beaming more positiveness out of my face and my chest and I am happy. I feel all right.

I feel like part of a community now which is wonderful and have met so many wonderful trans people. I feel supported and I feel like I've actually got something to share with people. I've got something to say. I've got a lot of stuff to say actually. I've always been a musician and this huge like block that I had in creativity is lifting because I've actually got that energy. I now know who I am and that's flowing a bit better. The best bit is that you arrive at a room and there isn't any music happening and then you all put your instruments on and then you play, then there's music happening and it's totally transportative. And then you finish and there's no music any more and it's like it's gone. It's amazing. Anyway, I'm quite a humble person, but if I go up on the stage and I don't show off, it'll be shit. So I have to show off a little bit, to carry it and it's just dead fun – more than anything.

Maeve

E-J

I like being able to just get on with my life - having a partner, having a job, doing my study, getting a First at university, and being at the museum. That's all I want to do. I want a nice career in the museum sector and I want to do my PhD and just be an academic, a design historian, a creative and skilled curator. I don't want trans to be much a part of that, but I don't deny that I'm trans. The example I try and set – maybe it's to myself as much as to anyone else – is that I'm an out functioning trans man who contributes to the important process of broader society learning more about itself through critical social analysis, understanding ourselves through historical investigations, or creatively through curatorial work.

My trans experiences have informed both who I am and my practice and there's no escaping that. I'm not sure that being trans actually defines me though. I don't like to think about it that often, I've spent too long already, wasted too much of my time, thinking about being trans, what it means, what it might mean. I like to just get on with my job. I don't need it to be the centre of my life.

The Brighton Museum and Art Gallery is an extraordinary place with an incredible collection and extremely informed staff. The place itself is going through so many difficulties because of the cuts in funding. I've been given an awful lot of training, and an awful lot of access to handling objects and my curator allows me to be part of the real workings of the museum. It's really important to me. I conduct a lot of investigations into local history, because I'm particularly interested in the history of Brighton. Not only as a queer space – I'm a dress historian, so it's always been a fashionable destination outside of London. It's where Beau Brummell – the world's first dandy who set trends here in England and in Paris at the height of the Regency era - partied with King George IV in the architecturally bizarre Pavilion George had just built.

Brighton has an extraordinary history and we all fit into that. It's changed my life, and because I'm so committed to the arts sector and the museum sector I've taken every opportunity that's been given to me here with great gusto and then hopefully given back to Brighton with the work that comes out of it. I've won grants, I've won scholarships, I've done all of this, I would say, because of losing ten years of my life to my trans experience. That's what's behind the enthusiasm and passion I've brought to my study at Brighton University.

I am gung-ho and drive myself really, really hard because having been trans not only interrupted my life it nearly took it from me. I am determined to achieve the very best I can no matter what. I will not let this life beat me again.

I'm the civilian LGBT liaison officer for Brighton Police so my role is to be supporting Sussex Police to do the right thing for the LGBT communities and also supporting the community in any interaction particularly regarding hate crimes and things like that. So I'm facilitating a two-way conversation. I'm that point of contact that people can go to. I think I'm the first trans person doing my particular job and I'm certainly the only out trans person in Sussex Police that I know of. I used to do trans awareness training with the Gender Trust and also with a LGBT project in town called MindOut. The LGBT liaison team of Sussex Police wanted to do more to support trans people and wanted to develop their understanding of the trans community and spread that developed understanding wider into the police service. So their colleagues actually do right by trans people.

They approached us at FTM Brighton to take part in a trans awareness training video and I got very involved and ended up being filmed delivering training directly to PC Rachel Piggott. It was a really fun project, and out of that I ended up getting a few contacts within the police. I was doing some other bits and bobs with them, about stop and search policies, again all through FTM Brighton. So when my predecessor was moving on to a different post she just gave me a call to say that the job's up and that maybe I should apply for it. I was unemployed at the time so I took that as a hint and I was very lucky to get it.

They say that trans activism is about twenty years behind that of the gay rights movement and I think there is an element of truth in that. There certainly has been more support towards trans causes in the past few years. It's a sort of natural progression; we're becoming more visible and we're getting more rights and people are actually beginning to take notice of us, giving us the space we need.

Rory

Sarah

I've written a children's picture book. It's brazenly about gender. It's aimed at children aged five to seven, because that's when studies show that children become aware of their gender. The main character I don't mention what their gender is, in fact the last page of the book is, are you a boy or a girl? I've deliberately made the whole book to be dripping with stereotypes and clichés about gender roles and identity and it's intended as a springboard for an adult or a teacher in a classroom, to start talking about what gender means to that child. A huge part of me wanted to write a transsexual children's book, in large letters, but I think I've done enough to get people's attention and not quite enough to really rile anybody.

Writing is an outlet for me. I write about myself, about stuff that's happening – about trans people in the media.

Something will fire me up and I'll just vomit onto a Word document and then I'll correct the swear words and publish it. I just stick it all on my own website. Sometimes it's about my past, sometimes it's about trans people being misrepresented in the media, sometimes it's just me writing a complaint letter, you know. I'm quite pleased with it actually. I looked at my year in review, and I've got about 40,000 views. I'm really pleased with that. Quite a few comments as well. Because I've got such a large social media following I guess, people listen to me. People read what I write, and they respect me and they take me seriously, which is something that I'd never, ever had before. This whole planning for the future thing is new, as well, because I never saw a future for me before I transitioned.

I'd like a more fulfilling life materially because I love cars and for the first time ever in my life, I want some kind of security in where I live. I don't know whatever it takes. If it's selling a load of books, so be it, or if it's finding a job and progressing through the ranks then that's what it'll be. I think an opportunity will present itself sooner or later and I'll make the most of it.

Gloria

I transitioned in May 2005. At the time I was buying hormones and blockers online and that went on for years. I lost my job because of that. I was successful in getting another job within a couple of months and the people I worked with were really understanding and just took me as I was then. I'm an Environmental Health consultant; I provide consultancy services to private clients. Principally food safety, but sometimes health and safety or communicable diseases based on almost thirty years of experience having worked in local government and the private sector.

I joined a local theatre group. My best friend who lived next door to me, her mother was really big in local theatre, and she persuaded me, bit by bit, to do stuff at the local theatre. "Oh come on, because we need somebody to do this" or what have you. And over a period of time I became a member of two or three of the local theatre companies and that kind of got me a social life. So, although I was working very hard, I actually did have a social life and I wasn't on my own any more, and my circle of friends started to widen and my interests started to widen. My life as a woman evolved over a period of time.

Luc

In this city, as elsewhere, I'm very conscious of 'giving back' to the community; I try to bring my own soul-saving visual (and recycling) creativity to the voluntary work that I do in relation to 'making ordinary' mental health, autism, physical disability and trans issues through the groups that I have joined.

I'm really enjoying, particularly in my less-mobile fifties, mobile 'phone-photography'. It's my own personal photojournalism, or photo diary. From the age of fourteen I wrote into little pocket diaries about my life, but that has stopped and now I photograph it. I've created one or two books from that, or I make what I call 'photo-videos'. For instance, my project over the last two years was collecting photographs inside disability-accessible toilets – but from the standpoint of being a transgenderqueer person. So, I snapped the doors, the taps, floors, toilet bowls, hand driers, tiles, plumbing pipes, etc.

For Trans Pride I fashioned for myself a trans lanyard: my 'tranny-lanny' or a 'well 'ard trans lanyard', and began photographing myself in the mirrors wearing this. I made a photovideo out of 250 plus still shots as a way of just light-heartedly showing a public some gender-neutral space: to trigger the question 'What does it mean for somebody to have to go and look for somewhere that doesn't decide whether they're male or female?" Obviously walking around in the streets, in the countryside, everywhere is gender-neutral in that respect. But if you go into non-charity shops or hotels, into schools or leisure centres, the changing rooms and toilets are divided gender-wise. Then of course you've got hospitals and prisons, etc. There's always this fundamental division about gender. I was playing with that issue to, hopefully and humorously, normalise and raise awareness about gender variance.

finally got work in Brighton through my friends, with whom I played Bridge, so after seven years of unemployment, I had a job. I would live as Jo, at the weekends, but at work I was John. And that sort of double-life, the stress was awful, very, very difficult. We managed until one Monday I came into work and had been out to a club the night before. I'd forgotten to take my eye make up off. I had no idea. I was just in a rush. I saw most people look at me. I just went into the loo, "Oh god." Took it off. Next day, my manager calls me into his office and says 'There's no easy way to say this, are you having a sex change?" Now, that's to the point, isn't it?

This was the end of 1999. Basically I had two options. I'd have to do what I've been doing all my life and lying and saying "No, this is not me, it's a mistake", or say "Yes, I want to become a woman". So I thought "Yes, I want to become a woman." He said, "Okay." I had visions at the moment of a P45. He said, "I've been and talked with HQ, and we have a policy. If you go to your doctor and get a letter that says you are transitioning to being a woman and undergoing treatment, we will support you one-hundred percent". At that point I broke down in tears, such a relief.

My colleagues at work were confused, but supportive, for the most part. There were two men there who were quite homophobic and so they started making nasty remarks. They also upset other women, because they were making sexist remarks about them. But when they started making remarks about me, they were called into my manager's office and they came out looking really downcast. They'd been given a good talking to, and he came up to me later and said, "How did you put up with all that?" I said, "Well, what am I supposed to do?" I said, "Thank you for standing up for me". He said, "If they give you any trouble, tell me."

In 2002, I left because I got a job offer as an Equality and Diversity Officer at the Learning and Skills Council. They actually valued me because of my experiences in diversity. I knew about the equality law, because I was reading up on it. I became a union activist in 2004 and I started talking to PCS Proud, the LGBT section of the PCS Union. I started going along to their meetings and I went to their AGM. And the previous trans rep stood down, so they were calling for people for trans rep. The Chair

turned round to me and said, "Jo, do you want to be our trans rep?" So I said, "Okay." That was 2005 and I'm still their trans rep to this day. This was something that I felt strongly about, encouraging other trans people, within the civil service to feel secure, confident knowing that they going to be supported.

Joanna

Sabah

I really want to stay in Brighton. I started really figuring out myself and doing stuff like trans activism and feminism here. I'm dreaming big already, like we all dream big at the start really. We didn't expect Trans Pride to be what it was last year, like it really blew us all away. The support and the atmosphere was amazing and so special. It really, really felt like it was our Pride. We have visions of taking over, like Queens Park or something, where it's got these beautiful landscapes. A really nice, friendly place, a really social place. And to have like different stages and to represent different parts of the community. Art tents and bring in more art and creativity. You know, creativity's important to a lot of trans people as an outlet and there are some brilliant performers and artists out there that just aren't recognised.

We should have a family area at Trans Pride. I think again people forget about trans people with families and whether they have trans kids or they're trans parents and stuff like that. It's really important to reach across to all those different groups, and probably have like a culture tent, yeah just to really celebrate all parts of our trans pride. That would be just so good.

Michelle

The work situation was another thing that really held me back from transitioning and coming out. I was very worried because there was no real knowledge of transgender at my work place. And I just was fortunate enough to come out to the right person, and basically just admit what was going on. I didn't really plan it. It just happened, as part of a chat. There was a conversation actually about trans people in Brighton, and I got upset, and one of my managers said, "Have we touched a nerve here?" And I said, "Well yeah, as it happens". And from there it was "Let's get HR involved. Let's talk about how we're going to sort this out". I took a day off work and I helped draft an email that they would send round, and the next day I came in and my inbox was full of happy emails and I think most people were generally quite accepting. Yeah I've transitioned at work with hardly any issues. Still doing quite a good job there I think.

Another thing that I've always done in my life is I've always been very much into music. I've been in several bands since I was young. Last year I started drumming for a band called Slum of Legs and that was great. Bashing a drum is the best thing to get things out of your system. We're an all-girl band and I've been truly accepted into that which is amazing.

I guess it's only been really now that I've started to use my personal trans history, expressing it through my art and through my creativity. I studied Theatre and Visual Art at Brighton University, which was a mixture of acting, performance and visual practice. After I graduated I realised what I really wanted to do was straight acting rather than just performance art type stuff. That is one very good thing about having transitioned: I can now play characters that, when I was at school, I couldn't. You know, there's only so many times I think when you're really young you can get away with asking if you can play a guy.

I've been doing stand up comedy for the last three or four years, and until this year, I had never mentioned the trans stuff, I guess because I wasn't out about it in my proper life. I actually did a stand up course in Brighton and that's how I got to know about the circuit and know other comedians in Brighton, and so on. When I did the beginners' course we had to find something that set us apart from all the other comedians; whether we felt it was a strength or a weakness or whatever. So obviously, at that point, I was like "Oh should I talk about the trans stuff? I don't know. It's comedy gold – why am I sitting on it? Why am I not using it?" But I just did not feel comfortable to start doing that at that stage in my transition or life.

Since becoming a member of FTM Brighton, and having a lot more to do with the trans community, I made the decision finally to start using my trans material in my stand up act. I did a couple of comedy gigs before I went on to perform in front of thousands at the very first Trans Pride, here in Brighton, last summer. The material went down so well. It was extremely empowering to do it and Trans Pride was one of the best gigs I've ever done. They had a big inflatable stage, and it was just such a lovely atmosphere and I did all the trans stuff. Of course they're going to laugh; a lot of the people there were trans or had something to do with the trans community, but I just felt so strong at that point; so empowered to be able to talk about all the stuff that I'd gone through.

The plan was to go on and use it at other gigs, but obviously there's a huge leap between doing it to an audience who can relate to the trans stuff and doing it to a usual audience in a pub, say. I guess I find that quite a scary step, but at the same time, I know other trans comedians who do it and are absolutely fine, and very successful. In a way, I think people don't heckle them so much because maybe they admire them and they respect them. So perhaps it's a good tool to use.

Ben

The only time I really performed any poetry before was quite a long while ago in Hastings. I was in something called an international poetry weekend. It was really good actually. And I took some poems to the first day of it and they let me read some. And I thought, "I've never done this before, but I'll do this". It was okay, they went down quite well; they were a little bit like the sort of stuff I do now, slightly political some of them and emotional stuff. The lady who was running it, afterwards, said to me "Oh, that was nice, will you come back tomorrow and do some more?" So I thought, "Oh great, yeah. I've been invited back." I was thinking of going back and just listening. So anyway I went and I remember getting to the door with my little clutch of poems in my hands, and I just thought, "I can't do this, that place is full of poets. And I went home. You see that's the old scaredy-cat I was and I feel like that sometimes now. But it feels real, I feel more honest now. I actually do feel it's okay to stand there because it's me and there is a difference.

I didn't realise I was speaking out for trans people particularly but I guess just by being there I was. I saw Verity Spott perform at the Komedia, the Poetry vs MC Slam, a few years ago. I was enormously in awe of her doing that. I was really warmed by the reaction of the audience to her when one of the rapper people made a caustic remark about her. The whole place, including all the sort of rapper fans and everyone – young people, old people, men, women, gay people – were just heart-warmingly on Verity's side. That's a big difference.

Alice

Ed

When I hear about young trans people I think about what it was like in my high school. Nobody, as far as I know, was out as gay, apart from one guy in the sixth form. Certainly nobody was out as trans. I don't think the school had any kind of policy about bathroom designation for trans students. When I was starting to explore stuff, going on the websites and the forums at twenty three, I was definitely at the younger end of the age range. There were some people that were eighteen, nineteen, twenty, but the majority of people were more like thirty and forty and starting off. Now people are figuring out that they're trans much younger. That change has only happened in ten years, that feels quite quick, it's great.

I'm glad people are coming out in high school and also that the other students seem to be really happy about it, and standing up for their trans friends – campaigning for them to be able to be kings and queens at the prom, and this kind of thing and it just seems wonderful. I wish I'd been able to do that when I was fifteen, sixteen. I'd love to have been king of the prom, not that we had a prom, but it would have just been wonderful.

I know it's been the sort of thing that often people bandy about – that the trans rights campaign is about thirty years behind the gay rights campaign. I suppose about ten years ago, the state of things for trans

people was maybe like the state of things for gay people in the 1960s. I don't know why that is. There is a snowball effect. More people come out as more television channels do documentaries or have trans characters. As there are more articles in the media, in a good way, then that leads to more people going to the gender clinics, more people coming out to their doctors and then that leads to more organisations having to have a policy to deal with that. That gets people talking about it and so on and so forth. So, it snowballs slowly.

It has felt, for me, like there's been a lot of stuff happening within the last five years. A lot of outrage now about the way the media treats trans people. No longer kind of just going, "Oh yeah, that's just what we have to put up with, that tabloid attitude." People are standing up and going "What the hell are you talking about, you can't say that, that's ridiculous."

I wrote a comedy drama pilot for the BBC Trans Comedy award last year and got long-listed but not short-listed. I was still very pleased that I did it. I'm hoping to develop it and keep working on it. I was also one of the photographers involved in the Queer in Brighton project. I kind of wanted to keep on going and do more about photography and representation. When I was involved with the Terence Higgins Trust we were producing a sexual health booklet aimed at trans people and we were trying to find people to be photographed but we weren't finding many people. So we said, "Shall we just do it ourselves? We can be photographed." It was a moment where I had to decide, "Okay, well if you do that that's being out in a quite different way from just telling a

few of your friends. You're on a booklet that's international." And so I decided the best thing I can do as a trans person, to combat the stigma, and the discrimination and the misinformation, and the snarky attitudes everywhere, is to be an out trans person. Then from there on I just thought of the more things that I could do in my life that raise awareness of trans stuff.

I hadn't really given much thought to writing trans stories and I think that was representative of the fact that I didn't always think of myself as a trans person. I thought of myself as just me, as Ed. I didn't really know how to grapple with my trans-ness. So I thought, "You need to write more about being trans and you will figure it out as you do it and you will produce something that'll be useful for other people as a result." So, that's my plan really, it's very much in its infancy, but my plan is to write for TV, to write books and write stories and enter competitions and do stuff about being trans, so that there's more stuff out there.

I guess normalising is the thing that I'm really aiming for here and that's why I think TV and film are important because people just take those in with their chips, you know, they're not really thinking about it. So if trans people are just there all the time on TV, eating chips as well, then hopefully it'll be quite a powerful thing over time. It takes a long time, but it could be powerful. That's quite removed from art galleries and small film festivals and things like that, which don't reach the masses. I'm very keen on reaching the masses. Not that there isn't a good role for all those art festivals and stuff, but no, that's what I want to do, reach the masses.

Taking part in that documentary, My Transsexual Summer, I didn't have a brilliant time with it. I was at the beginning of my transition and I was still very sensitive, vulnerable. None of my family or my partner wanted to be involved. The film company missed an opportunity to document the changes in my starting Testosterone. And when they cut what they had deemed 'my story' as an Artist in Residence at an Art Hotel (changing all my contact details to my new name), I felt written out of the documentary at a time when the social anxiety of initial transition was at its height. I was gutted.

I thought, "Right, how can I feel better about this situation?" Because I didn't feel they had represented me fairly. "I'm going to team up with my friend, Lewis", who was also on the show, "We're going to cut out the middle man and make documentary films about gender exactly how we want to." And that's what we did. I was lucky to win a large sum of money in a design competition, so I paid off some debts and bought really nice camera kit and audio equipment. We dived straight in, making our first film, 'Reuben'. Reuben and I share the same birthday, and we are a generation apart.

Thirteen months later Lew and I are working with All About Trans to produce twenty-five films, three minutes in length, of trans people all over the UK. Channel Four is holding our hands through the whole process. I find everyone's stories fascinating.

It feels good and organic taking things to that 'next level' and I love that we are already having endorsments from both the BBC and Ch 4. It amazes me that our only experience of making documentary film was first as subjects on mainstream TV, and then having the empathy and connections with the most wonderful people around us, our contributors, to make something special.

I learned as I went along how to film and edit. There's such a difference between the work I was producing two years ago and now. So much has happened for me career-wise as I've matured into myself, now 3+ years on testosterone.

I'm intrigued to see where My Genderation heads after this year. I see it an an ongoing project alongide whatever Lucky Tooth Films is sinking its teeth into.

I like the idea of being part of a wave of change and being the media source. It's much better when we do it ourselves and it's much more fun that way.

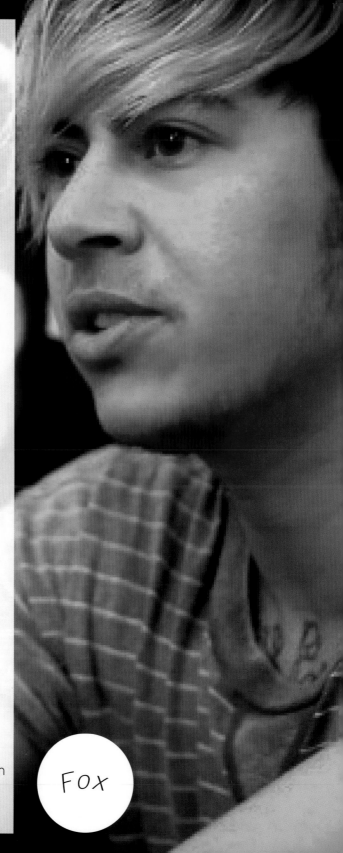

FOX

I've seen it move from the days that if I was seen outside dressed as a woman - there were policemen patrolling the streets in those days - I would have been put in the nick overnight. I'd have been brought before a magistrate in the morning, charged with offending public decency, and then probably sent off for medical treatment. This would have probably been electric shock treatment, which they called aversion therapy had I not had a family or something to rescue me from it.

I've gone from that age, when it was an unspoken sin, to now, where we have a freedom that was unimaginable back then. It's so heartening to see that society has become tolerant of something that's been there for centuries – at last to accept it. The Yogjakarta Principles were written sometime around 2001 and they are gradually seeping through into all the various things that we do. It was a marvellous conference that set up the principles that transgendered people should expect from society anywhere in the world. That was, if you like, the first stone that caused the ripples, and those ripples have come out and been picked up by society in places like Brighton. They will go further. In America there are cities that have established positive transgender policies, and they're doing brilliantly.

I am a public speaker at a lot of national meetings for older people's health and welfare. I never explain, I just get up and I talk. People are happy to listen to me and to accept me for whatever I happen to be to them. That is the example I'm hoping that we older trans people can set. Twenty years ago some people were black, some people were white. There was no question of anyone in between. If you had slightly darker features you were black and that was it. Now, it doesn't matter a bit. There are people of all sorts of shapes or colour and we don't care. We don't bother about it. All right, there's a few bigots around, but by and large society has accepted the fact that there are a whole lot of people of mixed race and that there are variants right the way through from white to black. It doesn't matter in the slightest.

Hopefully, we will bring about the same attitude of mind to the transgendered people in the next ten or twenty years. People will see somebody and it won't matter to them whether they're supposed to be a man or supposed to be a woman, or just something in between. Because there are people stuck in between, and they're the ones that are having difficulty.

Ruth

Sam

I think I am a bit of a maverick as a person. That's not why I'm transitioning but it's a good job that I have that characteristic because it keeps my head above water. Being prepared to break the mould and just be a little bit brave and go places where other people haven't been. We all stand on the shoulders of giants, don't we? And if we're prepared to do this stuff, then someone else won't have to in another twenty or thirty years' time and I really like that. Maybe having kids makes that more real as well, you know, I wouldn't want any of my children to go what I've been through, in terms of persecution. Or anyone else's kids that I know. Well, anyone. But I know some kids who are Christian who are clearly gay, or trans and I just thought they're not going to have the same struggles that I've had or the same rejection.

Steph

When I started out, transitioned twenty-one years ago, you were supposed to have your operations and your counselling and then just go away and just become a normal member of society. It's much easier now. There's many, many more of us who have put our head above the parapets. You would think you're the 'only trans in the village' type, now there's a lot more of us and we talk to each other and it's so much easier. Excluding the problems with Charing Cross, and gender identity pathway, it's so much easier now for trans people. Like when articles are published in the papers, people will turn up at mass demonstrations against certain writers and newspapers and notice will be taken.

I think one of the greatest examples of the power we have is the fact that the council did the trans equality scrutiny last year, and are still working on it. That was just something I never foresaw. It was a casual remark I made at one of the trans memorial days where there weren't any representatives from any of the local political parties. The Green Party wanted to have a word with us about it, and they suggested we have the scrutiny and if everything comes to fruition, it can make life in Brighton a hell of a lot easier for trans people.

I think we're moving towards more of a genderless society, but I don't think we're anywhere near it now. Gender as a whole has become less relevant than it used to be, because the wage gap and things like that are reducing, hopefully, eventually. Compared to my parents' time when they were younger. They said, "Oh, you know, you're lucky that you've been born now and you've been able to transition now because if that happened when we were younger, you would have just been labelled like you had something wrong with you. Or that you were a freak or something." So I'm thankful that we live in the contemporary world that we do, but we've got a long way to go.

Reuben

I hope things will get better because I had to hide myself away for years. My biggest hope is that children will be able to transition, will be able to block their puberty, before having to go through the level of pain that I had to go through. I will continue to suffer because of my body and that's really my key thing. It is not only to campaign for women who transition later in life, but also for the girls that are coming through today that are struggling with their gender identities and not being heard and not being recognised. And the importance of blocking testosterone early, because I've met trans girls, teenage girls who've had their testosterone blocked and what have you and I know that they live much better, much more fulfilling lives than I could possibly imagine. Just to look at them and know that they're not going to suffer the same level of distress or be treated so differently to every other woman, is something that's really, really important to me.

Rebecca

GLOSSARY

USEFUL TERMS

Androgyne
An individual who identifies as outside of the binary male/female gender identity; may be interpreted as indicating a neutral or a dual masculine/feminine gender identity (see also Genderqueer).

Asexual
A person may use the term asexual about themselves to imply that they choose not to be genitally sexual with others, whatever the understood sexuality or romantic attraction of the involved parties. Some persons may choose to identity as asexual in the A-Pride movement.

Anti-androgen
A drug that blocks the action of androgens (testosterone). Anti-androgens are prescribed to trans women as a means to suppress natural testosterone production thereby allowing the oestrogen that they are prescribed to be effective.

Asperger syndrome
Asperger syndrome (AS) and High Functioning Autism (HFA) are forms of Autism, a lifelong condition that affects how a person makes sense of the world, processes information and relates to and communicates with others. People with AS and HFA often have above average intelligence; this mostly hidden neuro-behavioural disability is known as a 'spectrum condition', as it affects people in different ways and to varying degrees.

There is known to be a 20% higher incidence of Asperger syndrome in the trans population.

Aspie
A colloquial term, used mostly by those with Aspergers, as either a noun to identify themselves and others 'on the spectrum' or as an adjective relating to their non-neuro-typical traits.

Binder / binding
Tight fitting vest or similar worn under clothing used to flatten breast tissue and create the appearance of a male chest.

Bi-phobia
Prejudice, discrimination, irrational fear, hatred, abuse etc. of bisexual people and people who do not conform to traditional ideas of straight or strictly homosexual norms.

Binary
Conforming to either one or the other of typical ideas of gender, sex or sexuality. A binary gender system assumes that gender can only be male or female.

BME communities
An acronym of Black and Minority Ethnic. A term used to describe and be inclusive of people from minority ethnic groups who are generally thought to have experienced racism and/or prejudice based on their skin colour, ethnic origins, cultural traditions, religious beliefs or practices.

Charing Cross
Informal name, due to its connection to Charing Cross Hospital, for the main NHS Gender Identity Clinic in London. This clinic is the oldest and largest clinic in the UK, which receives patients from all across the UK, many of whom are from Brighton.

Cisgender
Defines those whose gender assigned at birth matches their current/on-going gender identity within the male/female binary definitions. The opposite of transgender.

FTM: female-to-male
Trans man/a transsexual man. Someone assigned female at birth who intends to, is in transition towards, or has transitioned to a masculine gender.

Gender

One's internal sense of self as distinct from one's sex, which refers to specific physiology. A person's gender identity may match that of their sex (cis people) or may not (trans people).

Also with references to the socially constructed roles, behaviours, activities, and attributes that a given society considers appropriate for men and women. To 'gender' describes the act of one person, group of people or institution of assigning a gender role to another person or group of people.

Much of the social anxiety and pain felt by transgender people is due to being gendered by society in a way which does not fit their internal sense of their own gender.

Gender dysphoria

A recognised medical term which refers to the mental/social/physical discomfort of being perceived as and living as one's assigned gender at birth.

Genderqueer

An identity that does not conform to, abstains from, or goes beyond the male-female binary and stereotypical ideas of masculine and feminine. This also can be a political gender identity. Genderqueer can often mean different things to each person who chooses to use it for themselves.

GIC

Gender Identity Clinic.

HRT

Hormone Replacement Therapy. Some trans people choose to take hormones in order to help bring their bodies in line with their internal sense of gender. For trans masculine people this would be testosterone and for trans feminine people this would include an anti-androgen (see above) and oestrogen.

Homophobia

Prejudice, discrimination, irrational fear, hatred, abuse etc. of gay, lesbian, bi, queer and other non-straight identified people.

Intersex

Distinct from transgender, intersex encompasses a range of physical conditions that mean a human body does not fit neatly into the two biological sexes as perceived by Western medicine. Most intersex individuals undergo non-elective surgery and/or hormonal treatment in infancy and/or adolescence. Some intersex people may identify as transgender and/or choose to transition to another gender than that chosen for them by parents and/or medical professionals.

LGB, LGBT, LGBTQ, LGBTU

Lesbian, Gay, Bisexual, Transgender and Queer (sometimes the Q means 'questioning' in reference to someone who is exploring their sexual identity).

The T has been added to LGB in recent years and acknowledges that trans people suffer a lot of the same discrimination as lesbian, gay and bisexual people. The Q has been added even more recently. (See Queer Activism). The U, even newer, represents Unsure and is quite often used in relation to younger people.

Lower Surgery

Surgical process by which an individual's genitals can be altered to come in line with their preferred gender identity. Known as genital reconstructive surgery.

MTF: male-to-female

Trans woman/a transsexual woman. Someone assigned male at birth who intends to, is in transition towards, or has transitioned to a feminine gender.

Misogyny / misogynistic

Used to describe a sexist male-centric attitude. Misogynistic behaviour can manifest as objectification of women, discrimination against women, violence and sexual violence towards women and, in the case of trans people, the idea that they are not 'valid' in their gender identity. A lot of transphobia has misogyny at its root and affects trans men, trans women and non-binary people.

Non-binary
To not identify within the binary male or female ideologies in society. (See also Genderqueer).

OCD
Obsessive Compulsive Disorder. A disorder commonly associated with feelings and thoughts of anxiety, fear and stress. These can lead to compulsive behaviour and/or obsessive behaviour.

Oestrogen
Female hormone which some trans-feminine people are prescribed in order to gain female secondary sexual characteristics, including: breast growth, softening of skin, redistribution of body fat.

Packer / packing
An object worn in the crotch area by some trans men to create the appearance of male genitalia.

Passing
Being seen to be, or read as, the gender which a person chooses to present, e.g. a male identifying person being read as male by their appearance and mannerisms. Some trans people find this word to be problematic in that by 'passing' there is an inference that an individual has got away with a deception; which is not the case. It is not a deception if a person's trans status is not public knowledge as it is their story to tell as and when they see fit. The term also implies that there is a certain standard to which people must adhere in order to be viewed as valid within their gender, assigned or otherwise. This line of thinking can be harmful to cisgender people as well as those who are trans.

Phalloplasty
One of several options for genital reconstructive surgery which some trans masculine people choose to undergo, whereby a penis is constructed.

Pronouns
A preface expressing a person's gender identity. He, him, his; she, her, hers; they, them, their; hir, sie, ey, zie.

Queer
Can be a derogatory slur but also a reclaimed word. An umbrella term for those who do not identify according to heterosexual, homosexual or gender norms; a sexuality with a political edge, notably used in demonstrations "we're here, we're queer...".

Queer can often mean different things to the individuals who choose to use it for themselves.

Queer activism
Activism which promotes queer identities as positive and valid. Queer activists often try to subvert traditional views on sexuality and gender in order to promote a re-thinking and re-contextualisation of such. It is a politics which tries to resist definition and promote self-identification.

Sex
Refers to the biological and physiological characteristics that define men and women.

Sexuality
Sexual or romantic attraction to people, i.e. lesbian, gay, straight, bisexual, pansexual, asexual, queer etc.

Stealth
Living in one's acquired gender without anyone knowing about one's trans status.

T - Testosterone
Male hormone which some trans-masculine people are prescribed in order to gain male secondary sexual characteristics, including: a deeper voice, hair growth, increased muscle mass.

Top surgery
Surgery performed on the chest so as to bring someone's body in line with their gender identity. For trans men this can involve double mastectomy and reconstructive surgery and for trans women this typically involves breast augmentation.

Tranny

This can be a particularly problematic term. Historically it has been used in relation to transvestites (a term which is now largely redundant in favour of the term cross dresser). The problem arises largely when non-trans people use it to describe trans people.

Some trans people are comfortable with this but many trans people find it deeply upsetting and offensive. This is largely due to its use as a derogatory term, the implication of which is that trans people are playing at a role and that their gender identities are not as valid as those who were born cisgender. Some trans people use tranny as a reclaimed word, much like Queer. As a general rule of respect and etiquette, it is not advisable to use this term around people who you do not know to use it for themselves.

Trans

Currently-used umbrella term to describe all the varied identities within the spectrum. Formerly an abbreviation of transsexual and transgender, it also includes non-binary identities and those questioning their gender identity.

Trans*

Spoken as trans asterisk, or trans star; a relatively new term that has arisen via social media, used in place of 'trans' as an umbrella term. The * is not punctuation usage implying an explanatory footnote.

Transgender

An older umbrella term that encompasses various 'trans' identities (and experience), including transvestite, transsexual, trans-masculine/feminine, neutral, dual and genderqueer terms.

Transintersexual

An individual who transitions by hormonal and/or surgical intervention to be 'electively hermaproditic', i.e. to live as and identify as dual-gendered, embracing both male and female physiology.

Transition

The process of changing social identity and/or physical appearance in order to realise one's gender identity. Transition is a process which is personal to each individual and can take many forms, which can include: change of pronoun usage, name, style of dress and medical interventions such as hormones and surgery.

Transphobia

Prejudice, discrimination, irrational fear, hatred, abuse etc. of trans people and people who do not conform to traditional gender norms.

TQIA people

An acronym like LGBT but inclusive of Trans, Queer, Intersex and Asexual (see definitions). Can be added to LGBT as LGBTQIA in acknowledgement of more sexual and gender identities.

T-blockers

Testosterone blockers. (See also Anti-androgens).

Trans Pride

Three days of celebration and solidarity with and for trans people. The first event was in 2013 and the second in 2014, which featured the first Trans Pride march in Europe.

Trans Remembrance Day

Occurring annually on the 20th November the Transgender Day Of Remembrance (TDOR) is a day in which people gather worldwide to pay respect to and remember those trans people who have lost their lives as victims of hate crime in the preceding year. In Brighton members of the community generally gather at Dorset Gardens Methodist Church to listen to readings, light candles and pin the names of the dead to a memorial wall.

Vaginoplasty

Genital reconstructive surgery which some trans-feminine people choose to undergo where by the penis is inverted into the body to form a vagina, the festicles are removed and the skin is used to form labia.

RESOURCES

FULL **SUPPORT**

This is a list of online resources which may be helpful to trans people, their friends and / or families. It includes UK wide organisations and those based in London and in Sussex. A couple of these websites also include extensive links to further resources both UK wide and globally.

All About Trans

www.allabouttrans.org.uk
Project encouraging greater understanding between the media and transgender people in the UK, delivered by On Road Media.

Allsorts Youth Project

www.allsortsyouth.org.uk
Brighton-based support project for under 26 year olds who are lesbian, gay, bisexual, trans or unsure (LGBTU).

Assert

www.assertbh.org.uk
Brighton-based organisation supporting adults with Asperger syndrome or High Functioning Autism.

Clare Project

www.clareproject.org.uk
Brighton-based support group open to anyone wishing to explore issues around gender identity.

FTM Brighton

www.ftmbrighton.org.uk and
www.facebook.com/ftmbrighton
Social and peer support group for transgender men, gender queer people and those questioning their gender identity.

Gender Identity Research & Education Society

www.gires.org.uk
South East society providing information for trans people, their families and the professionals who care for them.

Gendered Intelligence

www.genderedintelligence.co.uk
London-based community interest company that engages and supports young people in debates about gender.

The Gender Trust

www.gendertrust.org.uk
National charity helping trans people and all those affected by gender identity issues.

Grassroots Suicide Prevention

www.prevent-suicide.org.uk
South East organisation supporting communities with training to prevent suicide. Not a crisis intervention service.

Mermaids

www.mermaidsuk.org.uk
UK national support group for children and teenagers with gender identity issues - also their families, etc.

MindOUT

www.mindout.org.uk
Brighton-based mental health service for LGBT people. Provides advice & information, advocacy, peer support groups / mentoring and web chats. Offers support with trans care pathways.

My Genderation

www.mygenderation.com
Sensitive & engaging documentary films exploring gender variance by Fox & Lew (Lucky Tooth Films), featuring many contributors to this book.

On Road Media

www.onroadmedia.org.uk
An organisation that works with excluded and misrepresented communities to look for solutions to social problems using the web, technology and the media.

Transiness

www.transiness.co.uk
A community website highlighting positive stories, good news and inspiration for gender variant and intersex people. Also has a Facebook page, search 'Transiness'.

The Art of Transliness

theartoftransliness.com
Tumblr blog with advice on life for the modern trans man and lots of links to other resources.